What the reviewers are sa[y] Live All Your Li[fe]

"While this book deals with the subject of aging, its greatest value is for those approaching retirement, and even for those many years from retirement, rather than for people already there. If read with an open mind, it can help individuals of all ages prepare now for later years."

Bookstore Journal

"Of all the recent books written about aging, this one is especially appealing. It is actually a book about graceful and creative *living,* aging included. Since Reuel Howe believes that aging is more a matter of attitude than of years, he addresses his book to all ages—young and old alike.

"He reexamines some of the incorrect beliefs we have inherited about old age and senility and suggests ways in which we can grow old gracefully, maintaining a vigorous and productive life. Highly recommended for young and old alike."

Mass–Media

"The author's name will command the topic to a legion of readers. Howe himself has escaped the malaise that affects many as their lives empty of purpose because their vocation disappears. But it is not the autobiography of a would-be retiree so much as the kind of creative chat that the retired and, especially, those far from retirement need in order to prepare themselves. A clear Christian viewpoint informs the counsel."

Christian Century

"Many persons will be helped through this book. It is to be highly recommended. Let it expand your horizons and make you a better and more fulfilled person. Excellent for church libraries."

Provident Book Finder

"At some time or other ministers want to recommend a title to one who suddenly feels the speeding years. There are many on the market but Reuel L. Howe's book is a thoughtful discussion of the entire aging process and how the passage of time, even in retirement years, can be a creative experience. Give this book to the next person who moans about the coming of age."

Christian Ministry

Live
All
Your Life

Reuel L. Howe

Word Books, Publisher

Waco, Texas

First Printing—October 1974
Second Printing—March 1975
First Paperback Printing—May 1976

LIVE ALL YOUR LIFE

ISBN #0-87680-853-4
Library of Congress catalog number: 74-82655

To make old age

a success, start young.

He is the happiest

who can see the connection

between the end and the beginning

of his life.

CONTENTS

PREFACE

This book grows out of my own experience of growing older, and out of my observations and study of what happens to others as they accumulate birthdays. Some people advance in years with the ability to adapt, grow, and increase their enthusiasm for living. Others give up quickly and surrender to decreasing interests and capacities. I have enjoyed assimilating each new year's experience into my growing sense of self and increasing power to be and to relate. I want to share my insights and observations with those younger people who are in the earlier stages of their pilgrimage.

This book itself flows out of my other books. *Creative Years* flowed into *Miracle of Dialogue,* which gave birth to *Survival Plus,* which now produces *Live All Your Life.* The theme of one's life expands and explores into new expressions as meaning adds to meaning, and the interaction of meanings gestates new meaning. All of us have a story which we add to each day. Awareness of that unfolding story makes it more possible for us to live our story more deliberately and daringly.

I want to thank many people who have participated in the preparation of this book. Peggy, my wife, by her literary and analytical abilities, has contributed enormously to the quality of what I have tried to do. Several readers contributed hours of time, energy, and thought toward the improvement of the theme and the writing: Sally Simmons, William McNamee, Margaret Chaney, and Marjorie Alpern. Finally, I am grateful to my secretary, Valeta Walters, for her assistance both as a reader who made valuable suggestions, and whose work on the manuscript made possible an earlier completion of it than I thought possible.

—REUEL L. HOWE

1

Perspective:
for Staying Younger
While Growing Older

"What are *you* doing here?" The question startled me.

"Why, what do you mean?" I asked surprised. "Why shouldn't I be here?"

"Because you're so much older than the rest of us," he answered. "What do you expect to get out of this workshop?"

I responded by saying, "I'm here because I want to grow, to keep my juices flowing."

"But how can you do that when you're so old?"

It was then that I realized I was probably twenty years older than the other people in the room. It had not occurred to me that there was anything unusual about my presence in the small group of seventeen people. I was simply looking forward to being a part of a weekend conference with some persons I did not know.

The leaders had not arrived yet and so I had been

watching the participants come in. I was fascinated by the different ways each made his or her entrance into the room. Some of the members stood or sat, a few chatted, others looked embarrassed or nonchalant, possibly disguising their uneasiness. I exchanged greetings with several as they passed by and sat down.

It was while waiting that I noticed the man who became my questioner. He stooped down and without introducing himself asked his abrupt and rude-sounding questions. Questions which made me feel that he resented my presence.

As the conference progressed it became apparent that, although still in his forties, he was afraid of growing old.

Periodically he would ask about my health and how I felt about being an old man. He asked if people treated me differently, and whether I found it hard to keep interested in things. Finally, he asked, "Do you have any fun any more?" Because I wasn't sure what he meant by that, I asked him to be more explicit and he said, "Well, do you have sex any more?"

In spite of my concern for this frightened man, I laughed. The intensity of his anxiety was seen in his anger that I should laugh at his question. I apologized, and then assured him that of course I enjoyed the pleasures and comforts of sex.

Somewhat appeased, he continued to press me from time to time with other questions about what it's like to grow old.

Because he was an active member of the group, and participated openly, he disclosed a great deal about himself. It became apparent that he was doing everything he could to hang on to his youth. He affected the dress of people much younger than himself; used a "with it" kind of language; and worked hard at cultivating relationships with the younger people in the group, especially the women. He continued to pay particular attention to me, possibly because in his estimation I was "old." I seemed to personify the age he feared, and he obviously was looking for every shred of reassurance and encouragement he could receive from me.

I felt like a pilgrim who was reaching back for the hand of a frightened fellow pilgrim who was very much afraid of what lay before him.

When the conference concluded, he thanked me for demonstrating that as he grew older—and he added, "as old as you are"—there could be possible satisfactions in his life. I am not at all sure he was as convinced as he tried to sound.

My fellow conferee was not unusual. Most, if not all, people, young and middle-aged, live in fear of growing older. And, of course, they fear losing the physical and mental powers they now enjoy with little or no awareness that different strengths and capacities can take their place. They do not realize that even present powers will continue to a modified degree, and that new gifts come with each age. Behind the fear of aging is the fear of dying: for some it is a frightening specter; for others, a part of life. Unfortunately, very little is done to either prepare people for aging when it's early enough to make a difference in how aging is experienced, or to help them mature in their feelings and perspectives about death. Our educating and nurturing institutions do not guide persons into a way of life in which they would be better prepared for both aging and death.

Fear of death, and the aging process that leads to it, is a common fear among us all—and we all have to make an adjustment to it. Much in our culture seduces us into believing that we are immortal. We are not even allowed to look middle-aged or older! For example, face, bottom, and breast lifts, bleaches and transplants all say, "You have to be young." Then the aged are hidden away; the sick are kept out of sight; and death is dressed up to look like life.

A Message for Younger People

My concern at this point is not with the aged and dying. There are many books on those aspects of life, but few that are concerned with the stages that lead to the end. My focus, therefore, is on you who are younger, even the very young who are making decisions and choosing ways of life that will influence the kind of aging you will experience in early, middle, and later years. I am offering here a message of how to live growingly; how to keep bodies, minds, and emotions alive no matter how long you live; how to age so that when the end comes you will know that you have experienced the deepest joys and sense of fulfillment that is possible. I am writing for you younger people who do not think of yourselves as aging but who are inexorably caught in the process and who need to know that, banning accidents, that you can determine how you will age and how you will end.

We can be the victims of falsehoods about aging. One is that as we grow older we find it more difficult to cope with change than we did when younger. The truth is that older people can be freer in responding to changing circumstances because of acquired perspective, patience, and realization that life is change. Another disabling untruth is that as we grow older we have more mental disorders than do younger people. Studies reveal that this is not true. Then there is the fear of senility which is not an inevitable condition, and is often caused by the fear of it. These myths are demonstrably untrue. If we allow these falsehoods to haunt us during our earlier years we will be building expectations to which we are more likely to fall prey. On the contrary, the freer we are from the influence of these myths, the freer we are to do our own aging in our own way.

Need for Preparation

Preparing for aging is like making an investment. When I invest money I am planning for the future. When I buy stocks, bonds, real estate, or whatever, I hope for good dividends and profitable capital gains. So it is in aging. As early as possible in our life span we can make decisions and choose a way of life that will yield good returns and increases in value; each year may add dividends of growing interest and increasing productivity and personal satisfactions. On the other hand, it is possible for a person to live his earlier years heedlessly so that when he comes to the end of life, he finds that he not only has lost his original gift, but has no dividends or profits because he spent all that he had for immediate gratification.

A Personal View

I am writing at the age of sixty-eight, two years from the allotted three score and ten. I feel qualified to write this book because I have lived with a growing awareness of what it means to live. Like the rest of us, I have been a baby, child, adolescent, a middle-aged person, and now I have moved into more advanced years. Each age has its own task, meanings, changes, and frontiers. I have lived responsively to some and drawn back from others. Each succeeding age both benefited from and was deprived by my responses to the former ones. When I was young, I did not see the interdependence of one stage of life with another, but now I do.

The difference between youth and age is that in youth we have a sense of immediacy without too much of a sense of the meaning of the past, and only a vague wondering about the future, except insofar as we may have been lucky or smart enough to make some choices and plans that might determine our future. In age, one has perspective. Life that at one time seemed so endless and so very immediate can be reviewed. Although one of the perils of aging is that one tends to reminisce and dwell too much on what has happened and lose the sense of immediacy that is so very important for keeping alive. While a sense of the past gives perspective to the present, a sense of a future can give added meaning and drive to a sense of the present. How important, therefore, to develop a sense of past and future in each age level. And this is true right up to the end of life.

When I was young it seemed inconceivable to me that I would ever be like some old people I knew: crabby, critical, and crippled in soul and body. And yet, there were a few elderly persons whom I loved, respected, and emulated. Actually, these people did not seem old. The more I came to know them, the less important seemed the age gap. In fact, I was surprised when one of my elderly friends died because I had not thought of him as old enough to die.

Now my turn has come to be old, and it seems unbelievable that I am as old as I am. When very young, I would wonder in a vague way what it would be like to be seventy which then to me was an unreal possibility. I really did not expect to age or ever accumulate so many years. Nor did I then think that when I reached sixty-eight that I would feel as young as I do because I felt that youthfulness belonged only to the young. I now find that the older person can have feelings of youthfulness; that is, I feel both venerable and young. The young mostly feel young, but the old may feel both young *and* old.

The other day I was asked what I projected for myself in ten years. I would then be nearing eighty. I had to face the fact that ten years, at my age, is certainly a hypothetical possibility. Nevertheless, I responded by stating that I looked forward to breathing, working, thinking, feeling, and growing;

to completing some writing and some other projects; and humorously hoped that I might be a guru in a commune on a tropical shore. Even if I have only a few months or a year, the potentials in that much future are enough to add to the meaning of the present. Thus, the older person does have a sense of future. Archibald McLeish, the poet and man of affairs, said somewhere, "At eighty, you have to begin to look ahead." Perspective for the person who is growing old, at whatever age, means that he appreciates and learns from the past; he can take joy in the present; and he can still continue to build and plan for his life ahead.

I was seventeen when I first became aware of myself as a person who had a future, and therefore owned my own destiny. That first sense of creative identity has stayed with me during all my years and is with me even now. So much so that my image of myself is often of that seventeen-year-old youth with a life before me and with a sense of its possibilities. While my sense of self has grown and matured, yet, that initial sense of self remains. Consequently, when I look in the mirror I am surprised. Next, I am happy to look so much older and yet retain the best characteristics of youth. I enjoy my energy, enthusiasm, and capacities to grow; my interests and projects that are more numerous than I can accomplish; and my capacities to relate to and communicate with young and old. I am grateful; grateful that somehow I found a way of life that retains an innovative and creative spirit in an aging body, and can enjoy the blend of wisdom and joy of life that is most precious. And even my body apparently does not appear as old as my years because it is sustained and energized by my capacity to love and give myself to persons and causes.

It is my belief that old age is often controllable and that we can sometimes influence the character and results of aging. To be sure, there are physiological changes, diseases, and accidents before which we may sooner or later have to bow. Although I have to accept these as they occur, I can also keep vigor going by exercise, and by development of new interests. Risking what I have for the sake of growth is another way. A friend, for example, risked whatever peace of mind she had by daring to take a desired course that she was afraid she might flunk. As long as I remain a self-conscious, vital self, refusing to be a captive of my fears, and responsive to my feelings and my environment, I can have remarkable powers to animate my body, change my emotions, ignite my ideas, improve and enjoy my environment.

Some Theories About Growing Older

Most theories of aging seem to fall into one of two basic camps. "Is aging nothing more than an accumulation of insults that the body is exposed to during its life span?" asked Baltimore researcher Dr. Charles Barrows. "Or is it built into the genetic material of the cells?" By "insults" is meant, the constant pounding received from the environment ranging from cosmic conditions to misfortunes, quarrels, and other forms of wear and tear. If this chipping away is the ultimate cause of old age, then people may be able to extend their lives and improve its quality by protecting themselves better. Learning how to protect oneself from the destructive assaults of life is one of the aims of this book.

The other theory about aging is that the genetic structure and vitality of the body deteriorates. Research is seeking to find ways to slow down the deterioration if not prevent it. It becomes increasingly clear, however, that we do have power by our ability to weather the stresses and strains of life, and by our generation of interests and creativity to determine how far, within those genetic limits, we may grow and be productive.

There are two possibilities for the aging person: he may

mature and grow in grace and power of relationship; or he may deteriorate and dehumanize. Either response may gain the ascendency over the person. If growth and maturation of powers increase, the losses that often accompany aging may be slowed and lessened even to the very end. In contrast, if deterioration of interests and purpose takes over, the symptoms of aging increase and become pervasive to the point where the person, be he young or old, is prematurely aged. With birth we begin the short or long journey toward death. At any time, from infancy on, we are old enough to die. And aging, which in some of its aspects must precede death except in cases of accidents that snuff out life, begins imperceptibly. The first years, from birth to the middle twenties, are characterized by steady growth and acquisition of increasingly vigorous physical and mental powers, knowledge and skills, with increasing vigor. Then aging begins.

Dr. Nathan W. Shock, Director of the United States Gerontology Research Center in Baltimore, Maryland, reports, "The first general finding in gerontology is that the body dies a little every day." Researchers report that aging is a gentle decline that begins around the thirtieth birthday. Apparently, human abilities do not face any sudden drop at sixty-five or any other age. The output of the heart and the speed of nerve impulses diminish by about the same amount between the ages of sixty and seventy as they do between thirty and forty. There is little reason to fear or even notice the declines of the sixties, anymore than the slight weakening of powers between thirty and forty.

Since the process of aging begins early, the preparation and planning of one's life for creative aging should begin then if not before. Actually, the foundations for creative aging begin in the early years of an individual's life. During these years home, school, the church, and other influences that are self-conscious about what they are doing in relation to children, need to be aware that they are nurturing and educating not only for the youngs' immediate tasks, but for the way in which they are going to move through the various stages of their life cycle. It may come as a surprise to some parents and teachers that the care of their children has a great deal to do with how those very same children will age some ten, twenty, or even seventy years later. For example, a child who acquires a low sense of self-worth in his early years and is unable to change it, has acquired an attitude toward himself that could lead to a process of defensive and crippling aging. A true sense of one's self is indispensable for moving creatively through all ages of life. A good beginning can lead to a good end.

Obviously, aging is a relative matter. Some people age very rapidly and early lose much of their power for further growth and maintenance of life. Others may live to seventy and beyond and remain healthy and vigorous. These are always people who maintain interests, outlets, and purposes that renew them. They need not be famous as in the case of Pablo Casals who continued a productive and notable career until the end of his life at ninety-six, but he is one dramatic example of how keeping active, both in mind and body, delays and compensates for the aging process.

This kind of achievement comes naturally for some, but for most people it calls for planning beginning in the earlier years of one's life. Preparation for retirement should begin long before the event. The man who is keeping in shape and acquiring new interests at the age of forty is already on his way to a successful retirement and creative aging. The possibilities for exciting living while the years accumulate should be kept open and nurtured.

The actual production by creative people shows that philosophers, inventors, historians, mathematicians, poets, musicians, writers, and many others who use their powers to create, retain their capacities for production in spite of evidence of waning capacities even into very advanced years. The same is true for ordinary persons whose continued growth and creativity do not make them famous.

The realization that many people remain vigorously active into what is normally called old age leads to two questions: are these people so active in later years because of their unusual vitality; or do they keep their vitality by staying so active? The probabilities are that we can say "yes" to both questions. The human system seems to respond to use and exercise, and since this is true, let us proceed on the assumption that by planning, decision making, learning, and growing, we may influence the character of our older years.

Finally, a basic concept of this book is our need of consciousness, of awareness of what we are experiencing from moment to moment. People who grow rich in the meaning of their lives are those who maintain consciousness of each moment in time, of each breath, of each day as an event to be lived and enjoyed. If we live fully and sensibly we will not look back with regret or ahead with fear.

2

The Pilgrimage From Birth to Life

While watching the plane being loaded in Winnipeg, I felt someone take the seat next to me. Soon I became aware of his looking at me and sensed that he wanted to talk, but I was not prepared for his question.

"What do you do?"

I turned and saw that my seat mate was looking at me with an engaging grin. "I hope you don't mind my asking," he added. "I enjoy talking as I travel. My name is Jim. I noticed that you are reading an unusual kind of book and I wondered if you would like to talk."

I did not want to tell him I was a clergyman because that information can produce a variety of responses which either lead to a termination of the conversation or into some heavy discussion about religion. Nor did I want to tell him I was a teacher because less and less I think of myself as a teacher, and more and more as a learner. Also, I find it very difficult to explain to people what it is I "teach." Again, I did not want to tell him I was an author because I was afraid he might think that that was pretentious. At least that is the way it would sound to me if I heard myself saying it.

He must have sensed my hesitation because he asked again, "What are you?"

I was surprised by my response: "I am a pilgrim." His face showed the surprise, and his response was not unexpected: "What the hell is that?"

Half jokingly I said, "Surely you know what a pilgrim is!"

"Oh, you mean one of those. Well, I thought they were all dead," thinking obviously of the pilgrim fathers with their tall black hats and white collars.

"I'm another kind of pilgrim."

"Well, what kind of pilgrim are you?"

"I'm a pilgrim who is trying to find the way from his birth to his life."

"Don't you mean from birth to death?"

"No," I replied. "I mean just what I said. I mean my pilgrimage from my birth to my life."

"Well," he responded, "where does death fit into your pilgrimage?"

"Oh, I expect to die," I assured him, "but life itself is a rhythm of life and death. In order to live, I have to learn to die; die to things in myself, surrender things I have for the sake of things I would like to have. The kind of pilgrim I'm talking about requires taking risks in order to have the kinds of experiences that keep me alive and going. I find I have to take chances, run risks, gamble what I have for the sake of what I want without any guarantees that I'm going to win."

Jim asked if I could give him an illustration of what I meant. I told him that some years ago I had a dream or a vision of something I wanted to try out. To do so would require that I resign from a very secure position where I was sure I could provide for my family, and where I had all of the assurances of a reputation already established. There were no guarantees that if I undertook the new project it would succeed; indeed, many people told me it could not and should not. After a long struggle within myself, repeated consultations with all sorts of people, and prayer, I finally decided to take the chance. I had to die to the security of my old position and risk the insecurity of the new project. And with that I had to risk the security of my family and the reputation of my professional career.

"How did your new project turn out?"

"Very well," I replied. "Much better than I had expected. That's one of the exciting things about being a pilgrim; when you take a risk you hope for success, and sometimes what happens far exceeds your fondest wishes. The chances were just as good that my attempt to make my dream come true could have fallen flat on its face and been a failure. In that case I would have had to return to my former kind of job, if available. But that's what it's like to be a pilgrim."

The conversation with Jim continued during our flight to Calgary. Some of the rest of what passed between us is contained in the following paragraphs. Intrigued by the concept of being a pilgrim, he began to develop some awareness of his own pilgrimage.

As I look back on my life, I see that many times I was stumbling along in the dark, not knowing where I was going. Occasionally a light would break through and I could see and travel in a known direction with great determination. Again, the light would grow dim and then I would have to grope my way from decision to decision. There were times of feeling lost, times of fumbling, stumbling, and falling. Sometimes someone standing by would help me up, sometimes not.

Maybe I would have to pick myself up. I would often bump into others, or stumble over some fallen pilgrim; hopefully, I would have the thoughtfulness and courage to reach down and help him up. But preoccupation with myself has often, too, caused me to ignore and turn away from the plight of others. Other times I have gone off on a tangent, following a trail that came to a dead end and I've had to find my way back to what, hopefully, has been the main course of my life's pilgrimage. And sometimes, because I was tired, discouraged, or afraid, I've had to back-track until such time as I could either generate some new courage myself, or be encouraged by somebody else to move out again into some new frontier.

I remember at one point in our conversation that Jim asked at what age one's pilgrimage began.

Our pilgrimages begin when we are children, before we are aware of their beginnings. A child has purposes, is trying to find his way; he does not know, of course, who he is, and so one of the things he is building without knowing it is a sense of identity. At first, he borrows from his important people their image of him. And he may very well accept this as a tentative self-identity while he begins to work out his own identity, which all during his life he will be in the process of altering, growing, completing. And no matter how long he lives, the job of achieving his identity is never completed. My first clear-cut sense of identity occurred when I was seventeen. It was then I was able to say, "I am who I am, and my name is Reuel." Through the years, I have been able to make that affirmation repeatedly but with growing meanings. While the central core of my identity has remained the same, new experiences, new relationships, and new insights have made my sense of self more inclusive and given it expanding boundaries.

As we grow older we may become aware of the cycles of

life through which we pass. We begin to see the whole process of our life from beginning to end, and the interrelationships of one stage of life with another; the interrelationships of meaning, for example, between the experiences when we were sixteen with those at sixty, and all of the other stages in between. The traumatic disappointments when I was a teenager seemed to pull the curtain down on any kind of future, but now I can see that those batterings were necessary to force a sense of self-possessing survival strength. At one time I remember asking, "Why didn't the captain of the ship call as he promised he would to tell me that I could be a member of his crew that was scheduled to explore Alaskan waters?" When it became certain that the ship had sailed without me, I had to begin the slow rebuilding of my self-esteem and sense of purpose. At the time it seemed senseless; now I see that experience as an important part of my pilgrimage and of the story of my whole pilgrimage. My heart aches for the young man I was then because I remember his hurt, bitterness, and sense of emptiness; but the young man unknowingly was writing the story of the man I have become.

So an awareness of pilgrimage makes sense of what seemed at the moment to be only senseless and cruel events.

Everybody Is Afraid

A pilgrim is often afraid. I am surprised that other people are surprised that I am afraid, which tells me that they do not know and understand what it means to be human. Such ignorance and illusion exist because education, religion, and cultural expectations persuade us that the mature person is strong, confident, and self-sufficient. We are given little help to be aware that with strength goes weakness; with confidence goes insecurity; and with self-sufficiency, self-doubt. The brave man is not fearless; he is brave because of the way he

28

behaves in relation to his fear; he would not deny his fear.

I was brought up to believe that to be afraid was weakness, and that the last thing I was to do was to let anyone know that I was afraid. It has taken me years to accept that because I am human I am also vulnerable; and because other people are human, they are vulnerable too. We need, perhaps more than anything else, relationships in which we can share with one another our vulnerabilities. When we begin to share our fear, we begin to trust each other; and the more that trust grows, the less necessary and important seem our fears. Of course, I cannot share my fear and vulnerability with everybody, but at least I can admit it to myself and avoid the evils of pretension and the building of a façade that isolates me from myself and from others. Occasionally, I meet a fellow pilgrim with whom I can share this sense of vulnerability and with whom I can build a sense of trust. Actually, this is what the church is supposed to be: a fellowship of vulnerable human beings sharing with each other in such a way that they grow a trust and a faith that opens them to each other and to the God in their midst. So this dialogue, this to and fro within me between fear and trust, and whenever possible the sharing of this fear and trust with others who are in the same process, is a means by which I am kept alive, growing, and moving on my pilgrimage.

Risk Growth!

Some pilgrims are "frontiersmen," those who live on the frontiers of their lives. What is a frontier? A child's first step is a frontier. So is undertaking to learn a new skill; or leaning into a fear that had incarcerated one. We take steps to free ourselves by cultivating new attitudes and relationships; the challenge of a new opportunity that will call forth new tests of our abilities and skills; and, of course, each new day can be viewed as an unknown frontier for our exploration. Moving into new frontiers calls upon our willingness to risk.

What is risk? I risk when I live on the edge of my personal and social frontiers. And risking means expanding and extending those frontiers so that we and the world we live in become larger and more interesting. The meaning of life becomes more exciting and worth exploring. Persons were created to grow; a non-growing person is a contradiction. Something has happened to separate such a person from a part of him that is essential to his being human.

But frontiersmen are not the only kind of leaders. Other pilgrims are "homesteaders." People who, having achieved a certain growth and development, decide to cultivate the personal and social domains that they have staked out. In those domains it is also important for us to keep exploring and discovering the possibilities that are contained within that world we have chosen, and our relationship to it. Some homesteaders are afraid to develop their domain. Instead they allow their resources to lie fallow, and opportunities to pass them by year after year. Other homesteaders cultivate what they have, and build for themselves a life of experimentation and exploration within the limits that have been chosen by them.

The frontiersman, on the other hand, is one who launches out into the unknown, who expands the psychological and physical boundaries of inner and outer space. He opens up territory that homesteaders can later occupy and develop. Risk for both the frontiersman and homesteader is great; risks of getting lost, of being ridiculed, of being different, of resentment, of not finding what one is in search of, and not developing what one has.

Risking, therefore, can be both extensive and intensive, both qualitative and quantitative, reaching into new territory or moving within the limits of a prescribed area. In either case the risk-taker maximizes his possibilities of being a growing person.

I want to make clear at this point that in identifying risk as essential to growth, I am not recommending foolhardiness and recklessness. When I risk, I weigh the issues and all the factors involved—personal and otherwise—in order that I may know whether I want to risk. What I have is of value, and I want to hold and use it with care and discrimination; and yet, the old saying is true: "Nothing ventured, nothing gained."

We need to realize that "status-quoers" as well as "growers" may have been once motivated to grow but were slapped by fears that set them back. When we draw back from the risk involved in moving ahead we may be responding to fear; to fears that are within us, to fears that exist in our relationships, and to fears of adverse forces in our environment. Our vulnerability becomes so great that we are afraid to face anything threatening and destructive to our present condition.

Our sense of vulnerability may be increased or decreased by forces outside ourselves. Trusting and encouraging parents and teachers, for example, reinforce the trust and courage responses of children. Chronically critical and hostile persons strengthen our fear responses. Aspects of our psychological, social, political, and economic environment add to our inner struggle between fear and trust. Some of these forces encourage our retreat tendencies, others encourage our desire to trust and grow.

All that I have presented thus far has great relevance for aging during all stages of an individual's life. Our willingness to share, and to risk moving forward are the critical behaviors that decide whether growth and life are to be fostered and maintained. Mother Nature gives us our physical, mental, and emotional growth and development which unfolds through childhood, adolescence, and young adulthood to the time of reproduction, as if her only concern was to keep the human race going. After that, she seems to be disinterested in whether we live or die. Because we are creative and productive in other than reproductive ways, we have created a society and a way of life that is entirely of our own making; and have, therefore, created motives for our continued growth. Now, however, growth is no longer a gift! If we grow, we have to decide to grow. Growth requires that we risk what we have for the sake of what we would like to have, without any guarantee that we will succeed in finding it. As we grow older, it becomes harder to risk than it was when we were younger.

Fear vs. Trust

The diagram on the following page illustrates what I have just stated. On the left is the pull of fear; on the right, the pull of trust; in the middle between fear and trust is the question as to whether or not we will risk growth. The withdrawal from the possibilities of life is a fear response and is indicated by the line which moves back toward fear down into a cocoon-like structure. Here the fearful person lives out his increasingly miserable existence. Occupying this pseudo security he resents the change and growth of others.

Thus, fear causes us to turn our backs on life and walk away from it. Instead of looking for life we are looking for a place of security, which becomes increasingly a primary concern. A fearful person will sacrifice anything, any value, any person, for his own personal security. Therefore, he cannot be trusted. That is why he frantically builds all kinds of shelters for himself on his backward course that will strengthen his shaky security. He builds these out of what I

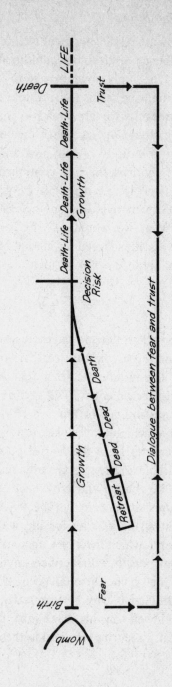

call "God scraps"—all sorts of odds and ends; convictions that have deteriorated into prejudices; old notions; old, old beliefs. Having built his cocoon, he peers out upon life defensively. He becomes impatient of any challenges that would threaten the flimsy basis for his dubious sense of safety. Fearful persons may either become rigid, dogmatic and bigoted; or, afraid to hold any convictions and are easily swayed by any stronger person.

Again referring to the diagram, observe that on the fear side of risk are the words "Dead–Death," which indicates that because this person has moved away from life in response to his fear he is dying or is dead and there is no future to his death. It is a dead-end death. The more he makes this kind of response the more he is trapped by it. Something may cause him to reverse his death course and begin to move again away from fear toward life. When this does happen, we need to be open to the possibility and be prepared to accept and help his turning from death to life.

Now let us turn our attention to the person who is moving through risk toward trust. He is willing to take risks and wants to move into more life. To move in this direction, however, he may have to give up or die to something that he has, for the sake of something that he wants, risking the possibility that he may not find it. This person is responding to trust rather than to fear. He trusts himself, he trusts other people, he trusts the possibilities in his situation, and he trusts exploring the unknown. Ultimately, of course, he trusts God. In other words, there is that in life which calls us to life, and the trusting person responds to that call.

You will notice that on the trust side of risk the word death is also found. The person who would move toward life must die, too, but his death is a doorway through which he passes in order to grow. Most of us have an experience of this movement through death to life. Perhaps it was when some important relationship was strained because of disagreements or misunderstandings that accumulated to the point of danger for both partners. We may be tempted, of course, to pretend that everything was all right and retreat from needed confrontation, and maintain status quo. Such evasion or pretense would be disastrous, especially if it became an habitual way of dealing with crises. But on those occasions when we faced the issue, accepted the pain, leaned into our fear and overcame it, trusted ourselves to others, let them trust us, and worked through to an understanding, we have had the experience of moving finally into a state of relationship which became deeper and more fulfilling than it had been before.

It is inevitable that there will be a succession of such death-life-death-life sequences in the course of our living. Each new and deepened stage of life brings us some new temptations, challenges, and conflicts. But as we have these successions of death-life-death-life experiences, we discover that our trust grows and our confidence and sense of security increases.

Effects of Fear and Trust

Even if our risking produces failure, we are stronger for having risked, for having trusted. Why? Because we dreamed a dream, marshalled our resources, opened ourselves to the counsel of others, tested our strength, and engaged in innovative behavior! But what about the failures? Many successes are often built out of failures and the lessons learned from them. The person who is willing to undertake creative risking may find other ways of bringing his dreams and purposes to fulfillment when his first efforts fail. But even if he never succeeds, he can continue to be an alive and fulfilled person because he can find joy in just being who he is. The fearful person, however, has little tolerance for stress, and often exhibits the effects of his fear in a variety of physical and emotional symptoms of illness. The person who responds to trust has a higher ability to endure stress without injury to his physical and emotional condition. He may live a very stressful life, and yet grow in self-strength, maintain good health, and pursue his purposes with vigor and increasing understanding.

Being on a real pilgrimage means therefore being afraid of life, of others, and for myself. Fear is an inevitable part of any person's pilgrimage: fear of failure; fear of being found out; fear of being real with people; fear of being inadequate. These fears paralyze my mind, dull my heart, and add weights to my feet when they are repressed and uncontrolled. Fears make me defensive; my response to them causes me more and more trouble within myself and between myself and others. When fear becomes chronic, it hastens aging so that we become prematurely old. Fear dries up our vital juices so that we become prematurely unimaginative and creaky. Fear can cause us to withdraw from our own pilgrimage and from the living of our story.

Our suppression of fear and kindred vulnerabilities has a destructive effect on our physiological, mental, and emotional powers. Continuing and habitual absorption of negative feelings promotes premature aging because they inhibit our breathing, increase muscular (including the heart muscle) tension, and interfere with digestive processes. A fear-denying pilgrim is apt to become a limping, incapacitated pilgrim.

The opposite of fear is trust. Trust pulls us forward whereas fear pulls us back. I am speaking of trust in oneself, trust in others, and trust in the healing and reuniting forces in life itself which gives us strength to fight against, if not overcome, the demonic that dwells in us and others. There is a unifying and releasing spirit that strengthens our own courage for living. When I trust, I am open, available, real, authentic, understanding, compassionate, and strong because I believe that trust puts us in touch with the whole of which we are a part of God. And it's my belief that a pilgrim lives between fear and trust; between their competing pulls, one back and one forward. Sometimes I am more fearful and defensive; at other times, I am more trusting and courageous. And I feel good about my pilgrimage when I keep my fear in dialogue with my trust, and my trust humbled by my fear. When this condition of dialogue between fear and trust exists, I sense that I am a better fellow pilgrim to others.

Dialogue Between Fear and Trust

Now for a little theological interpretation. The left side of the diagram illustrates the truth of what Jesus said: "He that seeks to save his life will lose it." The trust side of the diagram represents the other truth, "He that is willing to lose his life . . . will find it." We have here then, explained in human terms, the Christian death–resurrection rhythm of life as lived in response to fear and trust. There is also an added meaning here. Each experience of psychological, social, occupational, emotional, relational death is followed by life, and gives us training in dying as well as living. We may conclude from this that as we experience the death in living, we are being prepared for our final, physical death which becomes another act of trust and adventure.[1] We don't really know what is on the other side, but we trust; and our experiences of trust seem to teach us that death and life go together, and are the two parts of one process.

Some readers may think that I have drawn the responses to fear and trust too sharply and that no one completely fears

---

[1] See chapter 9.

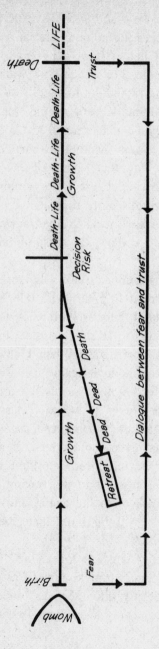

nor completely trusts—and I agree with them. A growing person never reaches the point where he does not know fear. When I was six, I had six-year-old fears which were real for me then, but simple. For example, I was afraid that when we went shopping I would get lost and would never be found. When I was six I had a very simple, naïve kind of trust: that my mother would take care of me, although I did have experiences of her not seeming to care because I became momentarily lost. Now that I am well into my sixties, I have sixty-year-old fears which are more sophisticated and complex. Also, my trust is more sophisticated and not as naïve as it used to be. I have to keep my fears in tension with my trust, and I have to allow my trust to be humbled by my fears.

Here is an illustration: Frank was badly hurt as a result of his being divorced from his wife. He had loved her and could not understand the reasons for her action. His response over the months was to gradually isolate himself from others for fear of being hurt again. When I saw him he said, "I don't ever want to risk love again." He was beginning to be captured by the fear motives in his life and in his situation. His retreat course needed to be stopped and he needed help in moving toward a more trusting response. Gradually he came to understand that even though he had loved and lost, he was stronger for having loved and that the worst thing a person can do to himself is to stop loving. Gradually he was able to take the risk of loving again, and was saved from a "dead death." He will be hurt again because, of course, to love is to be hurt.

Security is a big concern for us all. Frank was feeling vulnerable and wanted to make himself as secure as possible. When we look deeply into the lives of people who are responding more to fear than to trust we find that they are frantically trying to find and hold on to security. But they are not secure people. We cannot hold on to security. The more we try to hold on to it, the less we have. We cannot put it in a bank for reserve use.

On the other hand, when we look at the person who is living more in response to trust, who is risking and growing, we see a secure person. Such a person is not looking for security but for growth, and as he grows he becomes more secure. If we want to be secure we must spend whatever security we have in risk-growth possibilities. We possess security only because we invest it in our life ventures.

Some Important Questions

There is then the fear-trust continuum: the dialogue between fear and trust. And, as I have said, we all move from time to time back and forth between fear and trust. The question is which response is predominant in our lives, fear or trust? I respond to this question by asking three other questions:

1. Where are you in that continuum: more on the side of fear or trust?

2. Where would you like to be? If you are living on the fearful side, would you like to move out more toward the exploration of your unrealized possibilities? If you are hung up on an ambivalence between fear and trust, would you like to break out of that dead center and experience the satisfactions of more courageous living?

3. If so, what are you prepared to do about it? On one occasion when I was presenting these concepts to a group, an older gentleman, Mr. C., came to me during a recess with the remark that he saw himself and his attitude toward life well into the fear side of the diagram. He said, "In describing the fear response as leading to a 'dead death' you were

describing me. I suddenly saw myself; and I didn't like what I found. What can I do about it?"

"Can you identify any of your attitudes and actions that have put you there?" I asked.

"Yes," he replied. "As I grew older I tended to retreat from any kind of challenge or threat. I guess more and more I have wanted to play it safe. But I am beginning to see what it has done to me."

My response to his question, "What can I do?" was that he try practicing some opposite attitudes, open himself to feeling vulnerable, engage in encounters in which he would have to take some risks, and search for frontiers that he might again occupy. In short, try being a pilgrim again. Learn to love the road!

3

Living Your "Now"

Today is the doorway to the future. How I live today partly determines how I live tomorrow as well as the tomorrow forty years from now. Decisions that I make today build the basis of decisions for tomorrow. What I give to life today nurtures my capacity to give to life tomorrow. Today's investment may produce tomorrow's dividends. How to keep the investment market bullish rather than bearish is one of the great questions for investors, and is equally true for all of us in relation to how we grow older.

Pessimism vs. Hope

One of the dangers in growing older is the accumulation of feelings of despondency and cynicism. These conditions cause the market of living to go down and become depressed, even to the point of becoming permanently depressed. When we reach older years we are in peril of becoming prisoners

41

of hopelessness. One of the demons that stalks me on my pilgrimage is despair. Many times it has slowed me down and paralyzed my efforts to lend assistance to fellow pilgrims. The causes of this kind of despair are many. I am a major cause because in many situations and relationships I have disappointed myself by cowardice as well as by conscious refusal to face the challenges that have occurred in my life. My perception of the effect of this kind of behavior is that it has depressed my power to be. Another cause of despair is the disappointment I think I have experienced as the result of the behavior of others. Still another cause is the failure to accomplish goals to which I have given myself with probably unrealistic expectations, but the effect is the same.

And then I look at the political, economic, and social scene around me and it becomes easier and easier to succumb to the temptations of pessimism. I look for the ideal, and when I find the real I am not prepared to accept it because the real includes results that were not anticipated when I thought of the ideal. At the present time, the mood of despair prevails throughout our country, if not the world, and paralyzes. In every walk of life we may detect tendencies to depict only the wrongs of our world, and in the process existing problems loom so large that they seem to defy solution, so why look. And yet, the scandals of government, for example, are not going to invalidate the accomplishments of two centuries of our national history and should be regarded rather as proving the viability of political institutions. Our educational and religious institutions may exhibit he depressing effects of their preoccupation with organizational concerns rather than with the purposes of their existence, but the spirit of God and man can work together to rekindle hope and restate purposes that once again bring us to the new frontiers of possibility.

And so I fight despair with hope, pessimism with great expectation. Throughout my adult life I have continued to believe in man because I believe in God. The reading of human history reveals not only how cruel and destructive man is, but also how marvelous and creative. What fantastic things he can do with himself and with the world about him. What a summit and peak God has achieved in his creation. Always, however, we have to remember that along with our unlimited capacity for good, there is also our unlimited capacity for evil. Every one of us has, within himself, the possibilities of both. My power to love can become my power to hate. The longer I live the more I recognize within myself the potentiality for great evil. And I can understand with my heart as well as my head the crimes I hear about.

We have to choose between the good and the evil. Even when we choose the good we know that unwittingly we inevitably drag some evil with it because the good that we would do is never pure. Nor is the evil we do pure evil. Nevertheless, it is the choice that counts. And the kind of pilgrimage that helps aging to be creative is one in which we listen to the good that is in us, and try to respond to it. Therefore, I try to avoid despair and pessimism, because I recognize that they are killers. They kill hope, initiative, and a guiding purpose with which to keep life alive and moving toward a goal. To succumb to pessimism is to cop-out; to give way to deteriorating aging. Pessimism makes problems loom so large that there is no point in trying to do anything about them and, therefore, one is excused from making any effort. The moment one begins to stop making an effort, in that moment, one dies.

So, the biggest investment for the securing of a future is to keep trying, keep striving; avoid stopping and giving up the effort to stay alive. Resist the temptations to cop-out. Regard your pessimistic responses as mortal enemies, more to be feared than death itself, because they can produce in you a living death. At least when one is dead one does not pollute the atmosphere of hope. But the living dead, the despairing and negative person, makes worse what he deplores.

Another important investment for a future is the building of attitudes and responses of hope. Hope is the expectation of something that has not yet happened, but is within the range of possibility. It is the serum that protects one from infections of pessimism and despondency. More than an attitude, hope is acting as if what one hopes for is possible. It means doing something, and in the "doing" experiencing the movement toward fulfillment. At this very moment, for example, as I am writing, I am fighting feelings of despondency about being able to bring this book into being; but I keep going, I write, one word after another; and the very act of getting each word down engenders faint whisperings of hope that what I want to happen is happening. Such, at the present moment, is my investment in my future. The moral of this point for the aging is, the more one maintains attitudes and engages in actions of hope and expectation, the more one keeps alive; keeps the juices flowing and the creative energies renewing themselves.

Everyone wants to live a long life without boredom and with interest. But there are two problems: first, you have to grow old to do it; and second, you have to want to live. For many of America's twenty million citizens who make it past sixty-five the trouble seems hardly worth it. For them, old age is a time of anguish, loneliness, sadness, and poverty. For some, it is much worse than for others. For these reasons the temptations to pessimism are great. But granted the many problems, the possibilities for improved conditions for older persons are present and realizable.

Fighting Obsolescence

Back of the suffering of the aged is the tragedy of human obsolescence. Our society has a "throw away" mentality that is destructive not only to our natural resources, but to our human resources as well. Our "productive" and "marketing" psychology has room only for persons between the ages of twenty-five and sixty-five years. We fail, for example, to vote money for adequate education for children, and we shelve productive and creative people as soon as we can after fifty. Also, the rate of voluntary retirement is being set at ever earlier ages. Such a policy of obsolescence is robbing our society of talent and wisdom that conditions today indicate we need. I can remember times in my own younger years when I arrogantly put my objectives and point of view above those of senior persons only to realize later that I had something to learn and to benefit from them. Then came the day in my early forties when I realized that one day I must go that way too; that I would be a senior citizen, and that I would suffer from similar arrogance from those younger than I, and who are, in their turn, equally eager to push me out of the way.

Our marketing and technological society often dehumanizes the human. Even the in-people dehumanize themselves by rejecting both the younger and the older. I wonder if we will ever develop a human value standard to off-set the gross national product evaluation of human progress. My point is that the obsolescent mental set is disastrous both for society and the individual. All are its victims. It creates conditions that accelerate aging, and deprivation of power, position, and identity. Planned obsolescence as a way of life is life-denying because it robs all of a creative future. The practice of obsolescence promotes pessimism and despondency and discourages investment in any kind of future. What can be done to avoid discarding creative people in their time, and building a society in which persons will be encouraged to come into their mature fruition and find opportunities for expression?

One answer, of course, is to ask our business, educational, and religious institutions to change the situation by increasing their service to values other than marketing ones, namely, human ones. In all fairness we need to acknowledge that many in industry, education, and religion are already combating the dehumanizing effects of their respective institutions by developing policies and practices that also serve individual and social well-being.

The other answer can be supplied by the individual person. Try to live as to avoid becoming obsolete yourself; that is, stay current. As the person moves through the thirties, forties, fifties, sixties, he can prevent himself from becoming infected with a sense of personal disuse. How would I do it?

First, I would believe in my future. I am alive now and therefore I can be more alive tomorrow, even in the face of deprivations. Perhaps in a different way since we are versatile and are capable of inventing new forms for expression.

I have a friend of many years standing who, while he was rector of a large church, was discovered to have cancer of the throat. After removal of his vocal cords, he had to learn to talk in a new way. As he fought his own morale and speaking difficulties he volunteered to work with other patients who, having undergone the same operation, were often depressed and discouraged. Because of his indomitable courage his parish retained him as their chief pastor. Gradually, he mastered the techniques of forming words by the expulsion of air, and began to preach again with the aid of a chest mike, first only for a minute or two; then increasing the length of his sermons until he finally achieved full mastery of his power to preach although the quality of his voice was greatly diminished. He believed in his future in the face of great odds, and he invested in it by his determination to learn a new way of communicating and by sharing his courage and determination with others.

Another kind of overcoming is represented in the work of an early enforced retiree. Instead of succumbing to his disappointment, he volunteered his services to the government of his small city. After discussion of possibilities, he initiated programs for retirees and older people that became a spectacular success, and a model for other communities.

Second, I would believe in my own power of self-transcendence. That is, the power to surpass and excel myself. How can I climb out of myself and surpass what I am to become the more that I was created to be? The greatest prevention of obsolescence is to love and be loved. To love and be loved is to soar and soar and be free of the gravitational pull of the mundane and the impersonal. What kind of love do I mean? All kinds. Erotic love, shared in mutually, has its own power to energize and expand the boundaries of possibility.

This is especially true of self-giving love; loving because I was made to love, and because I am at my best when I give my self. One cannot love without increase of power to be, regardless of the response. My loving may be rejected or betrayed. I can be hurt and disappointed by the response, but nothing and no one can take away from me the increase I experience because I love. Therefore, when I love, I am investing in the future of my becoming; and, hopefully, in the future of the fulfillment of creation and contributing from our side to the completion of the work of redemption. Involvement in the work and joy of love is another way of fighting despondency, of transforming limitations that accrue from aging into new capacities, and of preventing the ravages of deteriorating aging from laying its at first gentle and later crushing hand on your body and soul.

Third, I believe that powerful as our institutions are, the individual person, singularly or with others, has power to change institutions and even to change the course of history. There are, of course, the spectacular instances of people like Winston Churchill who held a whole nation of people together by his personal power; like Einstein, who revolutionized the field of physics; like Martin Luther, challenging the rigidities of the Roman Catholic Church; and like Martin Luther King who, with others, began to bend the proud back of white racism.

There are also the private citizens, and groups such as Common Cause, who have power to change the nature and ways of organizations and institutions. I recall a layman who, with his family, became a member of a church that was badly divided with the minister caught between and immobilized by the two factions. When this layman arrived, the prospects for that church were far from good. After he realized how things were, he began to ask questions of leaders and the minister that helped them to refocus the issues. He quickly and subtly arranged informal meetings with antagonists who had not talked with each other for many months and sometimes years. He found youth and older people whose interests in worship and action were complementary and who, with him, worked within the two groups to break up the rigidities of feeling and thought. Gradually, a different spirit became manifest that began to release some of the creative resources of the congregation for love and growth rather than hate and conflict.

What relevance do these thoughts have for investing in your future? To believe in yourself, to feel, think, and act in behalf of your own self-respect, effectiveness, and the accomplishment of the humanization of organizations and institutions is to invest in your future and to keep your juices flowing, thus retarding your own obsolescence and premature aging.

A fifty-year-old clergyman, after attending a conference on Professional Development, was so turned on by his experience that he returned to his ministry with an enthusiasm that he had not felt for years. Apparently he communicated the effects of his peak experience so effectively that two members of his congregation wrote to me independently expressing their appreciation for the benefits that he had received and that were now being passed on to them. One wrote, "We thought he was finished—washed out and washed up. His creativity is available to him again and he both looks and acts younger." Some weeks later I received a letter from him in which he described the transformations he was experiencing in person, relationship, and work. "And you know," he wrote, "I feel ten years younger. Instead of dreading the years ahead I am looking forward to them."

These are the words of what had been a tired, defensive, defeated, prematurely aging fifty-year-old man. By attending that conference, and once again learning to believe in and trust himself and others, he made a huge investment in his future.

Time: Friend or Foe

Related to the issues of obsolescence and pessimism versus hope is the factor of time. And, obviously, time is an important consideration in our concern about today's investment for tomorrow's dividend in the aging process.

There are several attitudes toward time which create conditions of conflict between myself and events that sap my energies and diminish my self-respect and my self-control.

An important distinction is expressed in the question: is time my friend or my foe? It is my foe if I am constantly fighting it by racing the clock and trying to include in present time more than I am able to do. Under these conditions, my pleasure in the work I do is diminished and in its place I experience failure and frustration. The effect of this kind of battering on the person is to create physical and emotional preconditions favorable to aging. The opposite attitude toward time is positive: time is my friend. The heart of this more benign feeling for time is the realization that I can choose. I can choose from among many choices what I want; or I can choose to be driven and shattered by an inevitable flood of events. I can choose to be drowned by the downpour of "oughts" that descend upon us from all kinds of sources; or I can choose from among them what I want to do that will be in the best interest of others as well as myself. Of course, the choice is not a simple either/or, and the choices are not easy because when I choose to do one thing I have to choose not to do something else. So making time a friend in which life is to be enjoyed and one's being is to be realized means both choosing that to which I will or will not give myself.

I am thinking of a man of many wonderful talents and with a tremendous zest for life. He loves his family, his work, and is fascinated by many side interests. But he lives a frantic, driven, exhausted life that is further complicated by many minor infections and major fatigues. He expects more of himself than he is able to do; he is successful by the world's standards, but his own interior evaluation of himself is detrimental to his self-esteem. He is a slave to his engagement book which is a record of his driving sense of "ought" which turns all the potential joys and satisfactions into obligations which compete with each other. He is beginning to have serious cardiac symptoms and showing the effects of aging that are in excess of his years. He could choose what he really wants to do and eliminate some of the things he thinks he ought to do and begin to experience his time as a privilege and an opportunity. By so doing he would be investing in a more promising future. First, he is more apt to have one; second, it would give him more pleasure; and third, the toll of aging and its end effects could be reduced. To know oneself is the beginning of wisdom and of positive aging.

Discipline

The practice of self-discipline is a subject that naturally follows from our discussion of choosing. I am thinking of discipline in the sense that, in part at least, I cannot have any more than I give myself. The man described above cannot expect that anyone else will solve his problem. Others can only stand by and watch with sadness or joy as he chooses his own destruction or fulfillment. He can ask for companionship, counsel, and other helps, but his living is his own responsibility. He alone makes his investment in his future which will influence the kind of aging he will experience.

With this, however, must go another kind of discipline: the discipline of living the present for its own sake and not with an eye to what I am going to be or do in the future. What I am now saying seems contradictory to what I have been suggesting about investing in today for the benefits that might accrue later. Living in the present *is* an investment in the future if living in the present is real and not done for ulterior motives for future good. When I am listening to someone I can listen with the focus of my attention on what I will say in reply when he finishes speaking. The results for our future relationship will be disappointing because I was thinking about what I would say when he finishes (a future goal), and not about what he is saying now—a common cause of non-communication and therefore no relationship. Or, I can focus with full attention on what he is saying now, in this very moment. This is the moment of our meeting and I have forgotten the future, the character of which will be determined by the quality of our meeting now. So the investment that I am urging is the investment in the now. The business executive, who is our illustration, is anxious about his future because he is not disciplining his living in the here and now.

Living and enjoying the present is a way to invest in the future, and to re-create a changing aliveness with the passing years.

4
Cultivation of Creativity

What do I mean by "creativity"? I am indebted to the late Abraham H. Maslow's studies [1] for sparking not only my thought on this matter but my own creative responses as well. We tend to think of creativity in terms of products such as art works, bridges, buildings, writings, and other tangible evidences. Maslow distinguishes between the creative works and creative persons.[2] The latter he refers to as the primary creativity, and the products as secondary creativity. Children, for example, are creative but rarely produce any works worthy of preservation. Their creativity is stifled when some "teacher" requires them to copy a picture of a daffodil, or to copy a daffodil itself, and then grades the work on

---

[1] A. H. Maslow, *The Farther Reaches of Human Nature* (New York: Viking Press, 1971).

[2] A. H. Maslow, *Toward A Psychology of Being* (New York: Viking Press, 1968).

how technically accurate the drawing is. The product becomes more important than the person and how he sees a
daffodil. How much better it would be for the teacher to help
children to see, smell, and otherwise experience the daffodil
before suggesting they draw one. Our first task, therefore,
is to nurture our own and other's creativity, and to whatever
extent we succeed in becoming creative persons, everything
that we do will have marks of creativity. To be creative
is our first aim; to do creatively is the second.

I have also experienced this distinction and seen it in others.
Not until I became aware of myself as a creative person was
I able to produce creative works. Most of the thousands
of people that I have worked with in small groups do not
think of themselves as creative because they have not produced "works of art."

They have been educated to conform to expectations, to
be "right" rather than in relation, to distrust their own
thoughts, feelings and creative impulses. They relate to people
and situations with fear of disapproval and need to be ap-
proved. They revere the past and seek to pattern what they
do now on how men met their situations in the past.

When I invite members of a group to pair off, face each
other, put their hands palm to palm, close their eyes, and explore the space around them in response to music that cre-
scendos and diminishes, many of them move rigidly and un-
responsively to the music and to each other. The situation is
one in which I have suggested that they do a few things in
order to begin; there are many more responses that they could
make but they are obviously afraid to make them even though
I have not told them that they could not do them. For example, rarely does a couple move their feet, change positions
of the hands, push against each other or struggle, move with
different pace and intensity or really explore the space around

them, to name only a few possible variations. When asked how they felt about their performance, some responded by saying that they wanted to break out of their stereotyped behavior but were afraid to do it. They were afraid of what their partner would think; they feared doing something wrong; feared being embarrassed or causing embarrassment to others. When I asked what connections they saw between their response to the directions of the simple exercise and their usual behavior at home, some said that they live with their families and do their professional work with the same rigid, uptight, fearful, and unimaginative and uninnovative way. They are not able to be their real selves because they have been trained to deny the freedom to find out who they really are. Not only have they failed to cultivate their creative potentials as persons, but are unaware that they even have such potential. Their education has oppressed them and made them slaves to conformist expectations. This is a disastrous kind of education for people, especially for leaders who must not only find their own way like the rest of us, but guide us as we all face increasing obsolescence and technological, cultural, and personal change.

Toward the end of the conference it becomes apparent that some of the members are now more able to function independently and innovatively. When a suggestion is made they respond with more imagination and origination. Why do they and not others? Because they are the ones who have achieved a sense of self. What happened between the beginning and the end of the conference? The roots of the difference are found in the growth of trust between the members of the group which decreases fear and increases courage which means that some members especially are free to realize the creative possibilities that have always resided in them. They are now more their real selves and, therefore, are more creative. The same process by which a group of strangers learns to accept one another's sense of vulnerability, to trust one another and to become a supporting and challenging community, also releases the creative potential in those who are able to respond.

Cultivation of creativity could be the purpose of church and synagogue if the gods of conformity, convention, tradition, and legalism could be thrown out. Actually these institutions have a terrifying reputation for stifling the creative possibilities in people. It is also true that these same institutions have been the source of creativity in both lives and works. Where the spirit of the Lord is, there is freedom. Categories of belonging or not belonging, however, destroy the spirit and stifle creativity because "belonging" substitutes for "being." If we could only realize that "being" is its own "belonging." But every new movement that promises liberation develops an oppressive legalism that cramps the human spirit, once again attempts to incarcerate the Spirit, and thus begins a new oppressive orthodoxy. The most recent illustration of this tendency is to be found in some of the leaders of the current charismatic movement who often set themselves up to judge and exclude those who do not share their points of view. Those who have received the gift of tongues are "in" and those who have not are "out." They seem to ignore the other gifts of the Spirit that would equally qualify a person to be a part of the movement. Even the identification of themselves as a movement over against those who in their estimation are not, is a divisive act that contradicts their professed loyalty to the Holy Spirit whose purpose is to bring all men into union with Christ.

And yet, within the church, of course, there is trust, sharing of vulnerability, expectation of the novel, and delight in the original. Also to be found is resistance to the traditional which is the imposition upon us of yesterday's peak experience which is often turned into something suppressive and repressive. If we could only rediscover that wild, irrational love and joy that Jesus illustrated in the parable of the forgiving father. The father, disdaining the whole concept of cause and effect, ran to greet and forgive his erring son. So great was his pleasure at having him home again that he prevented his son from finishing his speech of repentance. The forgiving father was a creative father, one who prized being and relationship more than law, order, and obedience, in order to forgive.

Cultivation of creativity could also be the work of education. It could help the pupil become an authentic self, autonomous but in relation, disciplined but free. He could become familiar with history and its lessons and also aware of an understanding of the meaning of the present. He could be unafraid of novelty and change, and be free to grow.

Thus have I partially described a person of creativity. He lives in the present wholeheartedly; his "shoulds" and "oughts" give way to what he wants for self and others; he prefers to affirm rather than judge; he is spontaneous and yet when necessary he can weigh and be deliberate; he shares his fears, and surrenders defensiveness; he has courage and strength of his own convictions without need for being opinionated; he trusts with full awareness that he risks being betrayed; he does not need to control and is willing to trust his ability to improvise when confronted by something new; he is open to his own internal life as well as to the meanings that come to him from outside; when faced with a choice or decision he is not locked into the narrow either/or logic, but is free to consider many other options and, therefore, has wider choice possibilities; and finally, as a creative person he not only feels whole within himself, but feels himself to be in mystical union with the whole of life itself.

The creative person is given to expression rather than suppression and repression, and has therefore greater access to his own experience, impulses and imagery, conscious and unconscious. Openness to his own experience is an outstanding characteristic of the creative person. He is more candid about himself and the condition of his life; maintains more balance between masculinity and femininity—true of both men and women—revealing capacities for sensitivity and firmness, tenderness and strength, awareness and concentration. Finally, the creative person has a capacity to tolerate tension created in him by conflicting strong values. He has a liking for complexity, responds to challenges which call forth in him a need to correlate and unify multiplicity.

In some people these qualities are very strong and continue into their advanced years: such as the versatile and ever experimenting Pablo Picasso who died at ninety; the prolific "Jeeves" author, P. G. Wodehouse, who is still writing at ninety; Robert Stolz, a friend of Johann Strauss, is still composing at ninety-one. There are reasons for thinking that creative people do live a little longer than others; but, more importantly, the quality of their living seems far superior to those whose creativity has never been released; or who, for any number of reasons, have allowed it to be buried.

We now come to the question: How can we cultivate the basic creativity? The answer to this question will effect the accelerating or retarding of the aging process because creativity has a generative, maintaining, and renewing effect on one's energies and capacities for living. The answer to the question of how we can cultivate our creative potential will appear in the following chapters.

My last observation here is that foundations are laid for retirement during the earlier years when we are concentrating on living fully each moment, responding to changes and challenges, and developing our powers of versatility and origination.

One of the exciting possibilities for people in their middle and later years, when the pressures of family and work begin to lessen, is to discover hitherto unknown creative resources and search for ways of expressing them. I believe that every person has potential for being more creative. We have only to believe in and look for it. Learn to love being more creative.

5

Keeping in Touch With Your Body

Attitudes Toward the Body

In this life we are alive in our bodies. What life is apart from the body we do not know. And yet much of our training: parental, educational, and religious, succeeds in creating a condition of separation, if not alienation, from our bodies. Mind and spirit have been exalted above the body which has been minimized if not debased. We seek to develop our mental powers and our spiritual perceptions, but the health, grace, rhythms, and feelings of the body are all too often denied recognition. This continual denial of the meaning of the body operates on the face of the interdependence of body, mind, and spirit.

During our younger years many learn through unfortunate experiences and teaching to deny the body, and thus deprive it of its power to energize as well as express the vitality of

62

our feelings, thoughts, and dreams. Then in our older years these hitherto "guilty" bodies deteriorate, readily surrender to decay, and suffer breakdowns of function and use that ages us faster than necessary. The causes of our illness and disablement of older years may be in part due to the unrelieved stresses, conflicts, fears, unexpressed feelings and failure to correlate the life of body and mind. The failure to cultivate and express their interdependence and resourcefulness can spell disaster for the later years. We need, therefore, to get our whole "house" in order and functioning as early as possible in order to keep all systems energized and productive of more life for ourselves and others. Since the body is the vehicle of our existence, knowledge and care of, and reverence for the body is essential to becoming fully functioning persons.

Along with thousands and thousands of others, I was taught very early to distrust my body and to regard it as the enemy. Feeding, bathing, and resting were the only permissible positive actions toward it; otherwise, it was a source of evil and danger to my soul.

And yet, my body and the bodies of others, male and female, fascinated me. As a child the mystery of my body intrigued me. I experienced not only the enjoyment but the wonder of eating. What happened to the food? How did food become energy? Why did being hungry hurt so much? Then, I loved to look at my body and any others that might accidentally be available. I loved the feel of my body, and the changes it underwent. Soon I became aware of the wonderful feelings that seemed to center in my genitals and, at times, became diffused over my whole body. Later occurred the first puberty orgasm when my sense of power and ecstasy was followed by a sense of profound loneliness and incompleteness.

Accompanying all these experiences of wonder and curiosity were scolding, punishment, and accusations of sin and threats of disease. Wonder and awe were replaced by guilt and shame. The beautiful sense of self-discovery and awareness of being a part of life with its feelings of closeness with God disappeared. Without understanding it a sense of estrangement from my body began to occur, and it was years before my body and I could again be friends. For years enmity with my body complicated my development as a whole person, produced a sense of being unacceptable, impaired my capacity for entering into relationship, and finally, produced a respiratory illness that seriously threatened my very life. So thorough was my denial of my body that I lost some of my power to breathe.

During those years I could not believe that God could love me and thus began a placating way of life in which "love" was given with the hope that I would receive love. Needless to say, it was an unworkable transaction. Without a sense of validity of what one is, how can an authentic sense of self be grown; and then, how can there be relationships of mutuality between self and God and man? I needed my body, and my body needed me. The sickness of my body and the sickness of my self was the same sickness; and healing could only come when body and soul could become allies and friends and achieve mutual respect, love, and care for each other.

Gradually the movement to reconciliation and integration occurred over the years with the help of a loving, accepting, forgiving wife who endured and gave much during the continuing pilgrimage. In the context of that sustaining relationship other relationships of all kinds—some glorious, others bitter, and still others tragic—I learned to disidentify myself from the destructive attitudes toward my body, and achieved a constructive reidentification that makes life richer and more meaningful in spite of the very obvious demonic influences that operate in all persons and institutions.

I have made this personal revelation not because I believe it is unique, but because I know so many others who have walked the same fearful, defensive pilgrimage with a divided self. Many of the people in the groups I have met withhold the same debasing attitude toward the body and its feelings while idolatrously exalting mind and thought. For these people life can be cold, impersonal, and lonely.

The irony is that these people profess the Christian faith that stresses the belief that God, the Eternal Spirit, *incarnated* himself in a man, Jesus of Nazareth. Incarnate means to embody; to take up residence in a human body. Further, this same Jesus accepted .and loved his body in a manner that attracted all kinds of people to him; he had eyes that saw, ears that heard; hands that healed; a body that loved the warmth and comfort of human affection both male and female; and when he made his great gift he surrendered his young, attractive, vital body to the rude and rough hands of his executioners and the cruel weight and strains of the cross. And then there is the mystery of the resurrection of the body. Men claim to have seen him and put their hands in the wounds of his body. Why, why have so many people responded to the *embodied* love with such fear and guilt about the body?

We naturally express comfort and healing with touch; affection with embracing; love with kissing and intercourse; and communicate in any form of speaking and writing, with the aid of the nonverbal. I have noticed in congregations where there is opposition to touching, as in passing the peace, that when people greet each other they reach out to touch and embrace without knowing it. It is impossible to be and express ourselves without acceptance and use of the body. And yet this use must be appropriate to the relationship and not forced and artificial. I dislike being hugged by anyone, man or woman, without meaning. Hugging for hugging's sake is no hug at all.

The new freedoms of expression need to be used cherishingly and discreetly because body language is so precious. It becomes even more precious as we grow older because we begin to lose the people upon whom we depend for the touch of love. Children grow up and leave home; close friends move, members of our families and other intimates die or drift away. Finally, the lonely aged are often best ministered to by holding a hand, touching a face, kissing a cheek, or standing close to them with an arm about them. People isolated by illness have the same needs. The body is the instrument for the giving and receiving of love. Even God had to find himself a body in order to make his love known.

We need to remember, too, the many people who live alone, who by choice or circumstance have not married and are without families. They too have bodies with feelings of love and loneliness. Too much of our attention is given to married couples and families and too little to singles who need help in keeping in touch with their bodies which are equally for them vehicles of existence.

The character of our aging as we move through our earlier, middle and later years, depends upon how we feel about the body we live in; how we care for it, and use it for expression.

Learn to Enjoy Your Body

How do you learn to take pleasure in your body so that it contributes to your growth, aliveness, and maturing? How can you live in your body so that you move toward a more satisfying sense of self? We believe that the body is a gift, a marvelous gift filled with awesome wonders that work miracles of maintenance, healing, and provide resources for realizing personal and social potential. We should, therefore, treat our bodies with reverence and exercise those disciplines that will release our life-giving powers.

BREATHING. The first and most important function is breathing. Life begins when we draw our first breath and ends when we draw our last. What kind of breathing do we do between the first and the last breaths? We do not breathe adequately and when we need to breathe more deeply because of stresses, we are apt to breathe more shallowly. Breathing is one of the many rhythms that constitute the life of the body; and the question is how completely do we give ourselves to that rhythm?

The work of breathing can be simply explained. When the blood leaves the heart for its journey through the body it is bright red and rich. When it returns to the heart it is blue and dull, and filled with all the impurities it has collected.

The heart then pumps this used blood into the lungs where it is purified. The cleansed blood is then returned to the heart which pumps it through the body again. During a twenty-four-hour period the lungs cleanse 35,000 pints of blood. Oxygen is the cleanser and the presence of oxygen depends upon breathing and the kind of air that is breathed.

In spite of its being so very important for the preservation of life and health, most of us do not know how to breathe. What should we know? It is important to breathe through the nostrils which filters the air; to breathe deeply, filling the chest, expanding the diaphragm, producing the feeling that air is being pushed deeper into the body than it actually is; and to exhale completely. Exhaling can last longer than inhaling, forcing the bad air out.

Breathe deeply when under stress. The tendency then is to hold the breath or breathe shallowly. Deeper breathing relieves muscular tension which reflects psychological conflicts. Children hold their breath when angry and thus learn to repress their feelings. This pattern is commonly continued into adulthood. We even say: "I'm so busy I don't have time to breathe." When such condition becomes chronic, the physical and emotional life is in serious danger.

Periodic deep breathing during the day can both relax and energize a person and avoid the otherwise inevitable accumulations of fatigue which can lead to a variety of illnesses. Adequate breathing releases feeling; repressed breathing represses feeling. One way to keep in touch with the body as the vehicle of our existence is to breathe deeply and well, be aware of our bodies as a part of ourselves, experience our good feelings and enjoy them.

Only in my later years did I realize fully the benefits and joys of correct breathing. Having had a respiratory disease in my twenties, I became afraid to breathe and suffered from fatigue, depression and anxiety all of which produced a variety of other disabling symptoms so that in achieving anything I had to overcome the many bad effects of shallow breathing. Now, forty years later, practicing the disciplines of yogic breathing, I feel stronger, younger, more vigorous, freer, and happier. In tense moments when I feel myself tighten up, a few deep breaths replaces possible fear and repression with restoration of poise and control. To breathe deeply is to be more vitally alive, to move freely, and to feel more fully.

I also associate breathing with devotion. When I am deep into it, the meaning of the words "breathe on me breath of God" are realized. And as breathing becomes quieter and I surrender myself to whatever may happen, I feel that I am "waiting upon the Lord." Sometimes he comes in amazing ways: through words that invade consciousness, through colors, symbols, images, fantasies that are "given" to me which sometimes I understand and at other times I do not. Again, nothing may happen of any note. But it is good to have been open to oxygen, life, presence, meaning and the sense of potential in which, during those moments, I feel immersed.

Sometimes I feel that I am breathing in the love of God and exhaling all the dark, evil, alienated parts of myself until gradually I am so cleansed that I am inhaling and exhaling the love of God so that I am now in a condition to give what I receive. These are like the conventional prayer experiences of adoration, confession, intercession, and thanksgiving except that they are nonverbal rather than verbal. After these moments I feel refreshed and empowered and in touch with myself, others, and God. So breathing can be a way of physical, mental, emotional, and spiritual well-being.

EXERCISE. There are two purposes for exercise: keeping fit, and getting into the pleasure of being in your body.

The rationale for keeping fit is well known and needs no justification. Unfortunately, in spite of our interest in sports, which for most people means being spectators, we are notoriously physically unfit people. There are many, of course, who walk, jog, swim, bicycle, play tennis, and engage in other fitness activities which give participants an experience of bodily pleasure and emotional well-being.

Another activity that means a great deal to me is yoga which gives benefits to body, mind, and soul through breathing and posturing. One of the advantages of yoga is that some aspects of it can be done at almost anytime or place. Yoga may be begun at any age. No matter what our age or condition, there are things one can do, and benefits to be gained. Many of us sit at desks all day and tend to fall into postures that cause shallow breathing, cramp all the internal organs, block circulation, and deform the spine. When inevitable fatigue and stiffness overtake us, it is a simple matter to sit up straight and breathe deeply several times; or, better still, to get up and move the tense parts of our bodies by doing such simple exercises that even people in the same office may not know what we are doing.

When possible, lie on the floor, tense and relax every part of your body, inhale deeply and exhale completely several times, and let go. As breathing becomes quieter you may feel the tensions in your body leave you and your mind and feelings begin to quiet. If you do this for as long as five minutes, you may find that you have drifted into a higher level of consciousness which may produce not only rest and renewal but insight, even solutions to problems you had been struggling for consciously. From this kind of experience one can return to work with a sense of exhilaration and a new sense of possibilities.

Exercise thus increases oxygen-carrying capacity which is the best single measure of vigor, reduces body fat and nervous tension, and improves heart and blood vessel function as well as arm and leg strength.

Exercise also gives pleasure—the pleasure of getting with, responding to, and strengthening body rhythms. Because life itself is rhythmic, a rhythmic body is fully alive. Many of us see our bodies from without as objects separated from ourselves which causes us to feel awkward and self-conscious. How wonderful it is to learn to experience one's body from within because the more aware we are of our body and our feelings, the more we are aware of ourselves and of our physical, mental, and emotional power. We become responsive persons and develop capacities for spontaneity and movement.

The aging person, whether in his thirties or sixties, needs as much of the vitality of all his parts as possible, and needs also to learn how to keep in touch and renew his vitality. When, however, he loses touch with the feelings in any part of his body, he is out of touch with some aspect of the condition of his self. Keeping in touch means keeping the connection between muscles and feelings. Tenseness of facial muscles is a symptom of stress. Being aware of that tenseness and the relaxing of those muscles can put one in touch with the meaning and cause of the tension.

Another aspect of the body's contribution to the whole person is the relation between motor skills and the growth and sustaining of mental power. Learning to use one's hands as in craftwork is refreshing to those whose work draws on mental and emotional resources. Physical activity brings change, relief, and renewal. Especially people whose heavy responsibilities put them under great stress find that participation in sports, practice of yoga, the development and use of motor skills not only reduce tensions, but stimulate their creative powers.

It is also true that brain power increases body power. The more active we keep our brains, the more we learn and satisfy our curiosity, the more alive and skillful we become and remain. The more we stimulate our brain through learning the more we stimulate the body and its power to live and act, which is a clue for optimum aging. The sooner we begin this kind of process the longer it will last. This could be called preventive aging.

The body that, year after year, is kept fully alive and functioning will, barring accidents, continue to serve its occupant with health, flexibility, and vigor. Here is an investment that can make an appreciable difference in the experiences of aging.

DIET. Obesity has long been known to shorten life expectancy and hamper the freedom and agility with which to live however much life one has. Someone [1] has said that if a magician could move a wand and eliminate all the obesity, you would probably increase the life span more than by any other means. Keeping weight down, most researchers agree, not only reduces the risk of heart disease, but may also prevent diabetes which is so common among older people. There are many diets, but the best plan is to eat less of what we normally eat provided our diet is adequate.

Vitamins not only supplement diet but can be taken to prevent and arrest infections and diseases. Unfortunately many physicians and dentists deny that the use of vitamins has beneficial effects, but there are many of us whose experience in the use of vitamin C at the rate of 500 milligrams a day for prevention, or massive doses when infection threatens, convinces us of the value of vitamin intake. There are other vitamins that can be taken with C that help to keep the body well and functioning.[2]

Breathing, exercise, and diet, along with routine medical care, will feed, discipline, renew, and keep flexible the body as it moves through the years. And since the person and the body are one, a vital body will contribute to the vitality of the person. Likewise, the vitality of the person keeps the body alive and sustaining.

SEX. I cannot write about keeping in touch with the body without reference to the body's sensuality, and a discussion of sexual expression as we move from youth to age. As you

---

[1] I cannot find the source of the comment, but I think a similar statement was made by Dr. Nathan Shock of the Gerontology Research Center.

[2] For further information on the use of vitamins see Adelle Davis, *Let's Eat Right to Keep Fit,* Signet, 1970.

may remember, the opening chapter began with an anecdote about a middle-aged man's fear that when he was old sex enjoyment would not be possible for him. The other side of this fear is held by many older people. They have sexual feelings and desires and often feel ashamed and guilty. They wonder whether they should have such desires because the media and other communications of our culture create the expectation that sex is only for the young, that when they get older they should put away such youthful activity and accept the "norms" for their advanced age. Children of older parents, as well as younger, are often embarrassed by their sexual interests and activities. Sexual interest on the part of a senior man or woman opens them to the accusation of being a "Dirty Old Man"(DOM) or a "Sexy Old Woman"(SOW). Why that accusation for the elderly and not for the young? We are having the same difficulty accepting the fact that older people have a sex life as we had accepting Freud's reporting of the existence of sexual desire and response in children.

Every day, 4000 more Americans reach the age of sixty-five and they can expect an average of fifteen more years of life. Many of the present 20 million people over sixty-five erroneously believe that sexual activity should decline to the point of ceasing, and that sexual exertion is injurious to health. They may, therefore, shut off feelings, and deprive themselves of an intimacy that they need more than ever.

The sexual suffering and confusion of our time would be alleviated if we could learn to be more accepting of the fact that sexual arousal and responses are normal for the human being from the beginning to the end of life, and that response is to be encouraged rather than suppressed and repressed. Sexual interest and activity is one way of keeping in touch and responsive to one's own body, but is also a way of keeping in touch through the body of the person who is our partner. Studies reveal that when activity is continued that builds on sexual capacity that activity can continue into advanced age. Observations indicate that sexual interest and activity can even increase in the later years.

Masters and Johnson's studies, including monitoring of sexual performance as well as interviewing, found that a man's capacity for erection and climax, and woman's capacity for orgasm, were slowed but not terminated by aging. A slower sexual response is not to be viewed as an indication that one has reached sexual bankruptcy and that sex activity should stop. Quite the opposite should be the case—it should be kept alive.

What do these insights mean for people who are in the earlier stages of aging which, if employed, will sustain them during the later stages of aging?

Work together to learn to accept the body as a source and means of pleasure, intimacy, and relationship. Develop awareness of your body and its feelings of pleasure. Sadly, many people are aware of their bodies only in relation to pains and discomforts. There are the pleasures of being aware of the different parts of your body, and caressing and loving your own body. In order to be erotic with another it is necessary to be responsive to your own erotic feelings. Be aware of the pleasure of a well-groomed body, but also of your naked body caressed by the air that surrounds you. Be aware of bathing your body and be open to, rather then stifle, the feelings that are awakened. Learn and practice the pleasures of intimacy which is the pleasure of living with others in special ways: the touch of the hand, bodily pressures, the intimacy of skin contact, caressing the loved one with your eyes, beholding the beauty that comes from within both the beholder and the beloved. There is the mutual stimulation of the caress which with a little thought, if not training, can graduate into a loving massage that provides a couple with the precious experience of cherishing and being cherished. Some may think I am being excessively physical in my recommendations, but no one, for example, can experience a loving massage without the meaning of it moving through the body to the soul. It can be a reverent, loving, healing laying-on-of-hands which, like other laying on of hands, is sacramental. The touch can be an outward expression of an inner love that graces the outer part of another, enriches, and heals the inner spirit.

Practice sexual intercourse in the larger context of other forms of sexual relationship. The slam-bang, goal-oriented union of the genitals that is aimed at orgasm practically guarantees a short life for the relationship. Missing in such a get-it-over-with-quick method is tenderness, appreciation of the other, reverence for the mystery of intimacy and union, learning to grow from one another, the deliciousness of savoring every breath, movement, touch, sight, taste, fragrance, and sound. In such ways one grows an aura of love that encloses the lovers in a luminous state of ecstasy which lifts them out of the drag of the mundane. Then, when the union of the body takes place, it becomes the focus of ineffable joint being that for the moment seems to complete creation. After the climax comes the awareness of transfiguration; the giving of thanks one to the other; the return to tenderness and cherishment; the murmured word that recalls the remembered eloquence of the nonverbal poetry of movement in giving and receiving. Growth in this kind of sexual relationship promises much for the partners as they add year to year. They will be in touch with their own and the other's body and soul, and grow in their relationship with God and man.

Discard concepts of what is normal. What you feel and do in response to your feelings in mutual relation to what your

partner feels and wants is normal for you both. There is no
law in love, for love is above the law. Alas for the persons who
would rather be right and proper than to stay in relation
and grow in it. Expressions of love call for the exercise of
imagination, the freedom to innovate, and the creation of
novelty of action and setting. Many relationships are killed
by boredom, suffocated in the ruts of behavior dug by zombie-
like hands of monstrous repetition. When behavior becomes
habitual it is rationalized as normal. Such living is devoted to
the maintenance of the ordinary and to suppression of the
creative and the extraordinary. All life, especially the life
of love, wants to explode out of restraints into new forms of
expression. When we open ourselves to the possibilities of
radical rediscoveries of meanings imprisoned in old forms
of our behavior, we can expect exciting reformations and
transformations of relationship.

How do we open ourselves to explosions and implosions
of vitality? When locked into a habitual form of behavior we
need to ask ourselves: Why am I doing what I am doing? How
does what I am doing feel to me? What would I like to
do? Am I willing to risk the change, especially in relation
to my partner or others? These are the kinds of questions that
release life forces so that they can alter or revolutionize our
stifling norms of behavior. Questions such as these have power
to change answers!

Yes, there is risk in loving radically and innovatingly, but
there is even greater risk in not doing so. We are faced with
the risk of choosing between obedience to old attitudes toward the body and its relation to the soul, and the risk of
letting the body be fully alive and respond to its feeling,
rhythms, and powers of expression. There is risk in letting
sensuality and spirituality dialogue with each other because
lust might take over love. But there is greater risk in not

allowing sensuality to be in dialogue with spirituality. Without the communication of the spirit, sensuality becomes exploitive of self and others; and without the address of sensuality, spirituality may become unreal and uncaring.

Importance of Body and Person for Aging

Such mutual relationship between body and person is important for aging at whatever age. As I have grown older I have learned to love my body and to stand in awe of its resilience and resourcefulness in spite of years of neglect and abuse. Its recuperative powers are amazing, even in later years the practice of things that I have described here rejuvenated my vitality and restored my functioning. One of the best illustrations of this truth is that when senile patients were given increased oxygen most of them showed a remarkable improvement of condition. They became more active, slept better, asked for newspapers and magazines to read, and also resumed the care of themselves and concern for others.

As I indicated earlier, I recognize that the relationship between the person and his body is one of dialogue and is a part of a necessary dialogue within oneself. By dialogue I mean a continued mutual address and response. If I cannot carry on a responsible dialogue within the parts of myself, I have no way of being in dialogue with others or The Other. Since dialogue calls for mutual respect and reverence, the practice of dialogue with my body through listening and responding to its communications puts me in touch with my body, and with all of creation. Included is a sense of sharing in and being in harmony with the Infinite. I keep remembering that God through his body made himself known to me and others. I believe that through my body my soul gives love to others and experiences savingly the love of others and of God. I believe, therefore, that I worship when I breathe, exercise, eat, dance, and increase the grace and power of the body. By worship I mean being open and responsive to that which beckons me into being and service. In my earlier years, my spiritual exercises required me to deny the body, to regard it as sinful, to punish it by fasting and other austerities. So disastrous was this practice to my spiritual life that I reduced my devotions to a minimum and nominal kind. To pray with the head and at the same time to abuse the body is hypocrisy, even blasphemy. The split in my sense of being was intolerable; my body began to achieve a compulsive and evil power, causing behaviors that distressed me and others. Now there is more unity and peace, and a strong sense of Presence abides. With this greater sense of wholeness I now can give myself to conventional forms of worship and devotion with more sense of relationship.

There is in every individual a young person and an old person. God calls to both. Sometimes he calls the young person in us to wake up and even fight the old person in us because the latter grows weary and cautious; but other times God calls the old person in us to use his perspective and wisdom to guide the young person in us. The youthfulness of spirit and body has gifts of challenge for us as we grow older; and the maturity of body and spirit has gifts of patience and the long view for those in the younger years of aging. So the message to both young and old is: Love your body!

6

Finding Your Self

The last chapter emphasized the importance of the body to the person or self. It seemed to be saying: "I am my body and I must be aware of it." Now, however, these next two chapters will say two additional things: "True, I have a body, but I am more than my body: I am my self, a person who lives in and through my body"; and second, "I am a self who is called by and who calls to other persons, and by this process we call one another into being." The instrument for this process of communication is the body; but the fruit of this dialogue transcends the body and maintains its vitality and its service to the self.

The bearing that these insights have on aging is that human life depends upon self-awareness and the capacity of each self to address and be addressed by other persons. When that dialogue is discontinued or breaks down, the self begins to diminish and die. Inevitably, it will drag the body with it into increasing decrepitude; and, in turn, the dying body will further drag down the self. The growth of the self and the dialogue of self with other selves energizes relationships and supports the vitality of the person in all functions.

Two illustrations come to mind. One, of a man whose life was devoted to the manipulation of things and whose identity was that of a manufacturer. Behind this activity lived a self which, during all his years, had never been recognized or cultivated. Nor did he seem to be aware of others' identities and justified his rude and domineering actions by production of commodities. When he retired he had no resources for living, for relationship, or for other means of expression. He soon became ill, depressed, increasingly impatient and quarrelsome. The bankruptcy and misery of his undeveloped self made him more sick in body, and his bodily ailments further depressed his ailing sense of self.

My other story is about a man who devoted his life to business, too. Midway in his long career, because of a series of crises, he became aware that he was a person—a self of whom he could become aware, and that this self of his influenced, and was influenced by, the other persons with whom he was associated; family, business, and others. He became aware of a marvelous personal world that existed behind the world of transactions, but which could influence that world. As the years passed, his interest and commitment to the interpersonal and social increased. When he retired at sixty-eight, his deepest interests continued even though he resigned from his job. His personal and social commitment kept him busy and alive, and he was supported by a body that was constantly renewed even though limitation occurred as he aged. He experienced what we might call "youthful aging," that is, he kept his interests and expressions alive far into his senior years.

Attitudes Toward Self

At least three common attitudes toward self are to be identified. There are, of course, many and varied combinations of these.

LOW SELF-ESTEEM. Most prevalent of all attitudes is *low self-esteem* and *low sense of self-worth*. I have found that this condition exists in most of the thousands of people that I have worked with at any depth. As one person put it very vividly: "No matter what I try or am asked to do, my self-doubt holds me back like a ball and chain. Because of it, everything I do takes extra effort because so much of my energy is used up dragging that damn thing around." Some people suffer from this condition more severely than others which either paralyzes their efforts to live creatively or diminishes their creativity. The former are so crippled that they have given up on any dreams they might have had; the latter, who still possess remnants of their creativity, are aware of their potential but are so frustrated they become depressed.

Joe was one of the former paralyzed people. He participated in a seminar group for five days by offering nothing and giving nothing. Again and again efforts were made to draw him in because he looked lonely and miserable. Finally, he said, "I haven't spoken because I don't feel that I have anything worth saying. I'd rather listen." In the exchange that followed he admitted that he was tired of listening and that he would like to contribute. He added that he felt inferior because of what he regarded as an inadequate education. He had always been timid and the few times he had tried to express himself people didn't listen to him. All this was said in a voice that was hardly audible. Someone asked him, "Who are you?" In a faint voice he said, "I am Joe." Back came the question addressed to him, "Say it again, only louder: Who are you?" And, with a little more voice, but still timid, came the same reply. This exchange continued until finally he stood with legs apart and shouted with great force, "I am Joe! I am Joe!" With that he collapsed and began to sob. The prison doors of inferiority that had held Joe captive for so many years had opened up and left him free to grow.

Even in a relationship of trust that was only temporary he began to overcome his fear and risk affirming his identity as a self worthy to be present and to be heard. His struggle for self-worth was not over, of course. During the rest of the conference he continued his struggle by learning to comment, question, and make suggestions. Since then I have learned that he chose a career, completed his education, and has begun to assume positions of leadership. He looks and acts like a different person. He is not a different person; he is the same one, only now he has a more worthy sense of self.

The crippling effects of low self-esteem on persons and their relationships to others and to their work are immeasurable: discouragement, despair, unrealized potential, loss of creativity. The effects slow down the psychosomatic flow of vitality and reduce the well-being of the person making him more of a prey to the external and internal forces that reinforce and accelerate the inevitable genetic decay, thus producing premature aging.

INFLATED SELF-ESTEEM. Ethel is convinced that she can do anything that she wants to do. She appears to be without any self-doubt, especially about her worth and ability. So full of herself is she, that she is insensitive to the needs and interests of others. The fruits of her talents are exaggerated and her faults are minimized. She remains blissfully unaware of her ignorances and deficiencies. Criticism is rejected and causes her to turn it onto her critics. She keeps all challenges at a distance and self-criticism is an impossibility for her. She has opinions about everything and is never wrong. She regards her tastes as artistically correct and loves to give the fruits of her "creativity" to friends and family, who almost always receive them with dismay.

Beneath this bravado-like sense of self-esteem and confidence is a surging sea of uncertainty which is so completely suppressed and repressed that none of it ever enters her consciousness. Her emotional stress does manifest itself in many illnesses and depressions. Her many suspicions about other people are probably projections of her own deeply buried self-doubt. She is not accessible to help, and to a possible journey back to a real and authentic sense of self-worth.

A RELATED SENSE OF SELF. We are now thinking about persons who combine self-question with self-affirmation. Jack is such a person. He is real in relation to himself, real in relation to others, and real in relation to the total situation in which he finds himself. He can accept his fear, vulnerability, and doubt; and appropriately, he can accept comfort, help, criticism, and encouragement. On the other hand, his threshold for action is low enough that he does not waste much of his energies wrestling with ambivalent feelings about his ability to undertake a task on his own initiative, or accept it at the request of another. He expects to engage in self-evaluation and accepts evaluation from others. He is aware of his ignorances and deficiencies; and equally aware of his competencies and resources. He expects inner and outer tension and conflict: inner, because there are many selves within him, some that complement each other, and others that fight and compete for supremacy; outer, because he is aware of real differences between his own and others' view and valuation of issues. He is aware of his sins and sincerely wants forgiveness; but he is equally capable of understanding, heroism, generosity, virtue, and the power to forgive. Toward the actualizing of such capacities we all seek to move. Those who respond to trust do so; those who respond to fear cannot.

A significant difference between the three attitudes toward self—deflated, inflated, related—is that Joe and Ethel are afraid of entering into experiences, especially strange ones, whereas Jack's relational self rejoices in experiences of all kinds and plunges into them with eagerness.

Beginnings of a Sense of Self

A baby has no sense of self, so far as we know. That sense begins in response to being loved and not being loved. When he is loved, his identity is one that says, "I am one who is cared for and loved." This is his dawning sense of self and the beginning of his capacity to trust. When he experiences not being loved, he will think of himself as one who is not cared for and loved. From this experience will come a sense of mistrust and fear. We all have mixed experiences of being loved and not being loved and acquire, quite naturally, a mixed sense of trust and mistrust.

On the strength of his growing trust-mistrust mixture, the baby begins to explore his world. He identifies with every person and thing he discovers, beginning with his mother through her body and himself through his body and the care of his bodily needs. Out of continued exploration and discovery he establishes his increasing identities in more and more complex ways. His sense of self is influenced by his relationship with father, mother, siblings, other family members, friends, teachers, peers; and by his experiences in relation to his own body, feelings, ideas, and skills. Accompanying this process is the question which is asked over and over again: "Who am I?" "What am I?" These questions continue to be asked through every stage of the life cycle from infancy to old age. The tension that grows out of the asking of these questions can move us to a clearer understanding of who we are; or may be more than we can handle and can result in crippling of the sense of self.

I am strongly convinced, however, that the beginning experiences of my life do not determine my end. I can begin with trust and courage and because of other experiences and my response to them, end with mistrust and fear. Or, mistrust and fear may be changed to trust and courage depending on other relationships and my response to them. Probably most people become lost in a state between trust and courage and mistrust and fear with inevitable ambivalences about their selves. The struggle between the desire to become and the fear of becoming that characterizes the lives of most of us cries out for resources that will help us to decide in favor of trusting and risking.

The self is a biological, psychological, and cultural being that interacts with personal and other aspects of its environment. The hope is that through this process of dialogue I will receive more and more answers to "Who am I?" kinds of questions; and, at the same time, out of a growing and open sense of my own identity, contribute to others' sense of being. Even as the child has to know his mother as the "thou" before he can know himself as an "I", he cannot enter into the highest relationships that he is capable of until he can say "I" with as much meaning as possible. Only the person who becomes a distinct self, a real person, is able to enter into full relation with other persons. A great relation exists only between real persons.

It is at this point that my self-identity struggle makes profound connection with the life, teaching, death, and resur-

86

rection of Jesus. He lived the tension between trust and mistrust, between courage and fear. His power to live such a strenuous life came from his sense of being loved, and, therefore, his power to love. It enabled him to live on the edge of an abyss of rejection and death; the abyss of being tempted in the desert to compromise himself; deny who he was by selling out to the seductions of demonic powers; the abyss of the agony of deciding whether to save himself or surrender himself to an ignominious death; and crossing the abyss of final acceptance of his destiny to be the "man for all men."

Here is the source of whatever trust, courage, and power I have with which to move through my own ambivalences toward risk, decision, and action. Each of us lives on the edge of our own abyss, the abyss that Joe faced when he finally gathered his courage and shouted, "I am Joe," and struggled with his fear to be the self he was created to be. Each of us has to answer the question: "What do I have that gives me the courage to face the darkness of fear and other threats to my being?" I have my sense of self identity that is built on relationships that have guided and do guide and sustain me. But I must also achieve my own independence of them.

The Process of Self Growth [1]

The achievement of self goes through three stages. The first stage is *identification,* which is a natural and inevitable process for us all, giving us our first sense of identity. The second stage is *disidentification,* which is an effort to distinguish between what is authentically myself and what is not. The third stage is *reidentification,* which is re-relating my newly focused true self to all that first gave me my initial sense of self. Now for some illustrations.

---

[1] I am indebted to Roberto Assagioli, M.D., *Psychosynthesis,* Viking Press, 1973, for the basis of my thought in this section.

IDENTIFICATION. Let's recall Joe who had such a low sense of self that he could not take his responsible part in a conference and was afraid even to say aloud, "I am Joe" with the sound and sense of conviction. Very early in his life he acquired a fear to be who he was. His first sense of identity was: "I am a nobody." "I am dumb." "Others aren't interested in what I might say." He acquired this low sense of self from a family setting in which he was denied permission to try out the kind of person he might be. Having no alternatives he accepted this meek, submissive, self-denying identity and lived with it for more than twenty years.

Many of us have had similar experiences. I grew up in a family where I was taught that it was better to listen to others than express my opinions with the result that I found it almost impossible to take my part in discussions. When a thought occurred to me I was afraid to express it for fear someone would laugh at me. This became a part of my original sense of self identity.

But original identification operates in other ways. My experiences in and with my body, for example, caused me to think of my self as my body. I became the slave of my body and was driven by desires and practices over which I had no control. Or, another example, I was dependent upon mother and father and could not conceive of my self apart from them with the result that my resentments of and rebellions against them often made me ill. Also, my original identification with God was that of judge who had nothing else to do but to watch for every wicked thing I did.

Not all original identifications are negative and destructive. I identified with my mother's and father's courage in the face of misfortunes. I identified with my body's joy in racing up and down the beach in the warm air and sun. On occasion, I identified with my wonderful sense of the nearness of the love of God, and with the sense of forgiveness that came to me from him through many persons.

Whether the original identifications, which we assume to be ourselves, are good or bad, we need to become independent of them. We come, therefore, to the next step in the growth of the self.

DISIDENTIFICATION. What this means is that I must learn to disidentify with all that gave me identity in order that I may realize myself as my self. Going back to Joe, he had to separate himself from the relationships that produced him. The group members helped him to realize that he was more than the timid, fearful Joe he had been; that he was a self worthy of speaking and being heard. He had to disidentify himself from what he had been and all that had produced that weak ineffectual self. When an adolescent boy rebels against his father whom he both loves and resents, he is engaged in the business of distinguishing himself from his father and saying, "I am other and more than your son. I am who I am. I must actualize myself as my own unique self." This achievement of a sense of self is not limited to adolescence—it's a lifelong process, and we can have a large say in the kind of person we become.

The same process of separation and individualization has to take place in response to all our original sources of identity. I have had to move, for instance, from the affirmation made in chapter 5, "I am my body," to "I am *more* than my body: I am my own self, a conscious center of being and power. I can observe my body, care for it, direct and exercise it. I am a self that has a body." Religiously, I have had to move from saying, "I am Christ's" to saying "I am myself and that is what he wants me to be." What good am I to anyone if I try to be what I am not? So I have had to disidentify with much of my earlier religious training because I found that my religious identities were unreal. One of the big mistakes that many spiritual teachers make is that they do not allow those they are guiding to disidentify with original relationships. The serious spiritual pilgrim is always having to go apart and sort out what is real and what is false. Jesus' temptations in the wilderness were his attempts to disidentify with messianic traditions and expectations in an effort to find out who he was and how he would live and work.

There is risk in this endeavor of individualization. I have to risk my original sense of security, and trust that I will find new sources of security. I have to have courage to stand alone and accept the fear, loneliness, and all threats to my effort to be who I am. The rebellious son who is fighting for his identity is often afraid, but he is facing that fear in order to meet his need for a more mature identity.

REIDENTIFICATION is a third stage of self growth. Returning to Joe, who found a self that he could own, be proud of, and affirm, he now faced the task of achieving a new relationship with his family, friends, his life, his education, and career possibilities. His realized self reowned all that was a part of his life in a new kind of relationship that was more self determined. No longer as timid and defensive, he was free to risk, decide and act; in other words, to get on with his own pilgrimage. A son who has realized his own selfness as independent and different from his father is now free as his own person to re-own his relationship to his father which will make it a more mutual one. Now that I realize my self as being more than my body, I can re-own my body as my servant, the vehicle of my existence. Having realized myself as my own true self, I am now free to give myself in a new and more responsible relationship to my God. Personally, I am now more comfortable in the realization that Jesus wants me to be Reuel in the fullest sense possible (rather than trying to be like Jesus) through whom his spirit is freer to work.

Therefore, we see that the emergence of the self moves through the three stages of (1) original identification by which the rudiments of the self begin to appear; (2) disidentification, by which we distinguish self from all that gave us our start; and (3) reidentification of the realized self in all relationships.

The continuation through the years of this threefold process would keep the self flexible and open and capable of growth even to the very end of life. No matter how long we live we have to give up old identities and build new ones. "The good old days," for example, cannot possibly be the good days for today. Childish religious concepts are not adequate for adult years. Parents have to disidentify and reidentify with their grown children in order to have a current relationship with them. Here is a way of growing older without becoming rigid.

Role of Education in the Growth of Self

There are two kinds of learning, and each produces opposite self-growth results. First, there is learning from experience; and, second, learning from what one is told. Experience provides what I call indigenous curriculum—the curriculum found in natural happenings; that is, what happens can be a source of learning. I say "can be" because we cannot count on a person learning from experience. Think for a moment about all the experience that people have had during the course of their lives from which they seem to learn very little. Learning from what happens is increased when the person having the experience is helped to reflect, identify, and formulate his learnings so that they may be available to him for incorporation into the growth of his self as well as of his knowledge and skill.

Jim and Sally's first two years of marriage were so destructive that they were becoming more and more estranged. A counselor helped them to think about their experiences together. By sharing with each other the effect they had on one another, they discovered that instead of each helping the other to become, each was damaging the resources of the other. Both of them were low in self-esteem. Sally didn't think she was loveable and sought excessive reassurances from Jim; Jim felt defensive in relation to women and was having trouble getting established in a new job, both fears expressing themselves in dominating attitudes and actions toward Sally. They learned how to relate to each other more supportingly. Together they formulated principles that guided them in new ways of living their relationship. The counselor did not tell them what to do. He guided their reflections on what happened to them in response to different kinds of behavior. He also helped them to share their fears and build their strengths for being independent as well as dependent selves.

Another way of thinking about the learning possibilities in experience is in terms of fate and destiny. What happens to me is fate. In the midst of the many happenings that overwhelm us, we may feel helpless, victims of fate. Not until we learn, as Jim and Sally did, to use what happens to us in ways that serve our creative purposes does fate become destiny and we are free to pursue our destiny. Out of this kind of learning we become authentic selves who stand on the solid ground of our own tested observations and the convictions that emerge from them. We achieve our own sense of relatedness to truth which is always dynamic because it is always born out of struggle, out of the wrestling between opposing principles; submission to fate and pursuit of destiny. Perhaps they would not use this kind of language to describe the change that occurred in their lives, but Jim and Sally embodied the effects of this kind of experiential learning.

The second source of learning is didactic, learning at the feet of someone who has the knowledge and who undertakes to give it to you. Certainly, there is a place for imparting information and knowledge although the student needs to be prepared for receiving it. Learning from experience and learning from instruction should work together. The laboratory work in a science course honors this mutual dependence. The shared authority of the student, and the authority of the teacher-learner in the dialogical process decreases the dependence of the student on the teacher and enables the student to achieve a real and integral relationship between himself and what he is learning.

Unfortunately, much education produces an opposite result. The institution, whether school or church, seeks to indoctrinate the learner, give him an accepted point of view along with knowledge. The real learning and understanding that the student may bring to his studies is more often than not ignored. Without much attempt to bring the new learning into dialogue with what he already possesses, the student is made a repository of what I call "layered education." Layer (subject matter) after layer (more subject matter) is laid on him without dialogue and, therefore, without his being able to correlate the old with the new. He becomes the victim of indoctrination. Instead of setting persons free to know, grow, and participate, this kind of education makes them slaves of accepted religious, political, economic, social, and other doctrines and conventions.

Education that enslaves produces anxiety-ridden, fearful, and defensive people who, lacking courage to face uncertainty and threats, retreat either into dogmatism or into hedonistic distractions of mindless entertainment. Both dogmatism and hedonism produces a low and powerless sense of self which will cause an acceleration of fears that intensify aging. Didactic education is always in danger of becoming education by domination, and, when it does, it inhibits creativity and growth of authentic selves.

Dialogical education liberates persons to be thoughtful, questioning, and affirming participants in their own lives and in the life of the world, and nurtures in them courage to risk, decide, and act. Courage is also the source of being and the growth of a sense of self worth. Courage likewise keeps the physical, mental, and emotional powers of the self focused and alive through the years in spite of illness, fatigue, discouragements, awareness of inevitable death, and the diminishment of powers due to advancing age. Dialogical education is entering into relation of student with teacher, and the two with truth. It is education out of love, and liberates persons for self growth.

The finding of self is dependent upon education that is as concerned for the growth of persons as for the transmission of knowledge and for technical training. We need help in learning to become compassionate, knowledgeable, and capable persons. All kinds and levels of education, therefore, can have a profound effect on how we choose to age, on our attitudes toward older people, and on our desire to provide more adequate resources for living the older years.

7

Giving Your Self

In the midst of one of my conferences a member of the group asked me privately, "What can I do to feel less alone?"

"What have you done to increase your sense of belonging?" I asked.

"Well, I've talked and tried to tell them about myself, my family, and my work, but I don't feel that I've gotten through to them."

"Have you listened to the others?" I queried.

"Of course," came the reply.

"But have you really heard? Perhaps some of your sense of aloneness comes from a preoccupation with yourself and inattentiveness to what you've been listening to. Try listening, really listening!"

Every person is alone—a solitary one. Each of us is born alone; much of our life, even when with others, is lived alone; and, of course, we die alone. Each person is a mystery that can never be fully plumbed. Out of our solitariness we seek one another over the abyss of the separation, uniqueness, and mystery of each person. "How can we reach each other?" is a deep human question. It can be a relevant one for all of us as we grow older because with advancing age we often lose the willingness to listen.

Giving Through Listening, Speaking, and Dealing

The two perpendicular lines in the diagram represent two selves, or persons, each alone but each reaching toward the other. The space between them represents the abyss—the separation that always exists. How can this abyss be bridged?

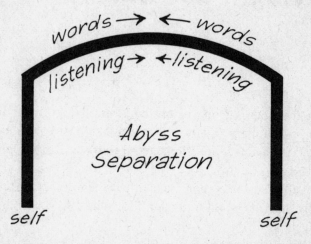

First, by listening. Listening, not speaking, is the initiating act of dialogue and, therefore, of relationship. Listening is the work of both seeing and hearing: The eyes hear the body language, the non-verbal; the ears hear the words. How true this is of a baby's seeing and hearing as he watches and listens to every move and word of the mother. Likewise, do we adults listen with both eyes and ears. Listening builds a bridge between persons; each side by its listening builds a bridge toward the other until the listening efforts meet. Over this bridge our words, the messengers of our separate but now bridged selves, may travel. Each person listens to the other and speaks out of self to the other. Thus is dialogue begun—but only begun. As this dialogue is continued each person hopefully is helped to become more himself and to be more in relation to the other one. Our two lives are interwoven with many other lives in all kinds of ways which both strengthen and complicate our relationship.

So far I have identified two steps in dialogue: (1) *listening,* and (2) *speaking,* but there is a third stage which will determine the outcome of our effort to bridge the abyss.

wrecks of hoped-for relationships

self   self

The third stage is to *deal* with the traffic that is crossing the bridge. The traffic of our messages to each other can be burdened and tangled with all kinds of meanings and feelings. If undealt with, the weight of them can become so heavy that the bridge collapses. We have to keep the traffic moving so it will not pile up. We keep it moving by dealing with what happens; by risking being hurt, unheard, misunderstood and unloved. We may, at times, have to risk our very selves. And when the bridge breaks, as it inevitably does sometimes, we start building it again, sending our verbal and nonverbal messages across and dealing more realistically with the traffic of meanings as it builds up again. Thus the self grows out of dialogue that accepts and copes with its content no matter how difficult and threatening.

The self that is forged out of bridgebuilding and repairing, out of *listening, speaking,* and *dealing,* acquires a power to be and to survive. Another insight gives encouragement to us as we grow older: The aging of a self-respecting self that has built strong bridges of relationship with others and who has respected his own and others' self boundaries, will age with a sense of identity, with grace, and with continuing resourcefulness.

Recently, I watched a television program about an eighty-year-old woman teaching chess to a group of teen-agers. Frail, but full of vitality that made her eyes sparkle, she taught chess and talked with them about life and values. She talked about her own youth and relation with her parents, about parents in general, revealing understanding of both teen-agers and their parents. She listened and responded to questions with understanding, raised her own questions in a non-judgmental way, and gave them realistic affirmations of themselves as persons and as a group. She presented a beautiful picture of a frail but very alive, interested and responsive person. She did not come by these qualities accidentally. She acquired them by her own struggle to keep alive, believing, and loving.

By listening, speaking, dealing, she kept her self identities flexible and growing. As she grew older and passed through the various stages and episodes of her life, she had to repeatedly disidentify with identities that had served her, and reidentify her true self with the inevitable changes of relationship and circumstances. Thus, she became an open, interested and responsive older person, a truly centered self capable of dialogue with young and old.

Giving in Spite of Distractions

Our central self has many competitors that exist within our own self universe. An illustration will help me make clear what I mean. All through the years I have been conscious of the growth of my central self in response to all my experiences. My central self is the one with which I address myself to the opportunities and responsibilities of my life. It is my coping and creative self. But I am still aware that I have competitors within me that distract and scatter my energies. They are "satellite" selves that rotate around my core-self blocking the realization of my full potential. Early in life, for example, I acquired a depreciating self that was so strong it threatened at one time to immobilize my power to grow and be creative. I also have a guilty self that tends to make me feel responsible for every breakdown of relationship. There is also my paranoid self that causes me to blame others rather than facing my own responsibilities. These and other satellite selves take away my energy and ability to relate and function. My task has been to be aware of these and seek to pull them into my center, and transform them into sources of energy for constructive rather than destructive action.

An interesting but disturbing question is, how can I unify my self-universe? I have discussed the importance of dialogue in relation to others. Now I stress dialogue within myself. Dialogue between my central self and the fragments of myself is both possible and essential. A self divided against itself shall surely fall and drag the person down with it even to the grave.

Any dialogue takes courage, and certainly dialogue with

oneself. Recently, a part of my work has not succeeded as well as I had hoped. The failure is a source of personal embarrassment to me because it looked to me as if I were losing face in the estimation of others. Both my depreciating and guilty selves combined to threaten my core self and my powers to deal realistically with the situation. With the aid of others, I have had to dialogue with these distracting satellite selves, identify them for what they are, what they are doing to me, and consider what I can do to bring them into my center—not as distractors, but as energizers.

My temptation is to surrender to these competitors and distractors which would ultimately bring deterioration to my whole person, body and soul. Such a process accounts for the frustration, fear, irritability, and isolation of people as they grow older. Let me explain further what I mean: failure, approval of others, criticism, and rejection are all distractors which feed upon my satellite selves and can obstruct the growth and development of my central self. For instance, if I have dealt successfully with my depreciating satellite self, I can dare to risk failure; and if I fail, I can look at the failure, learn from it, pick up and go on without demoralization. It is a great feeling when I realize that I have not lost my whole self because of a failure. Or, if I am consciously aware, for example, that I have a satellite of low self-esteem, I am able to become less dependent upon the approval of everybody; or the need to be liked by everybody; or the need to conform to what others think I should think, feel, or do. Or if I realize that I have a satellite self of guilt, I will not blame myself for not measuring up to perfection. If I have discovered that I have a paranoid satellite self, which is inclined to blame others for my weaknesses, failures, and errors, I will be able to understand why my relationships with others are so often strained and short-lived.

These are all examples of what I mean by "satellite selves," the selves which keep us from being real in relationship. Due to the fears and trust-mistrust relationships of our early years, all of us have developed satellite selves which distract us to one degree or another. Attempt to identify what your satellite selves are and how these selves might be distractors for you. Once they are recognized and accepted as part of you, they have essentially lost their power over you.

Recognition means that they are no longer free to distract and distort you without your knowing it. At the same time you may realize that you built these satellites out of needs that may not have been met. My "guilt satellite" may have been constructed in order to make me feel more comfortable with judgmental people in my life. I now realize that I do not need that kind of defense, that I am more than that guilty self that has been sapping my energy. So I begin to talk to it, argue with it, and gradually defuse its power to draw me into destructive behavior. As I continue this kind of dialogue within myself I begin to feel more affirmative and good about being who I am because the energy of that satellite is now a part of the reservoir of the energy of my creative self. Thus we are able to survive our years positively.

Giving in Spite of Fragmentation

The distractors operate within our inner selves. Fragmentation comes from outside of ourselves, which can consume us if we allow it. Our life is so complex that we are often besieged and battered by interests and demands and we can easily experience a fragmentation of our resources to cope with all of them. We are in danger of trying to respond to too much, and spread our attention and energies so thin that we are prevented from penetrating to the deeper and more sustaining meanings. The more superficially we live, the more sense of fragmentation we have and the more shallow our lives will become. When we live on a superficial level, we are more aware and affected by the fracturing, dividing, and disuniting forces. A deep strong sense of self enables us to break through life's fracturing, fragmenting forces and gain a perspective and a sense of sustaining purpose. The deeper one goes into the level of self-awareness and self-actualization, the more one begins to see, implicit in the fragments of life, a cohesion, a potential unity, an interrelationship.

Along with its scattering aspect, it is the nature of life to find its unity and to seek to come together. In the cohesion of the most elemental forms of nature, we see a prototype of love which has power to unite what is or seems diverse. The blowing wind, for example, scatters the seeds but also distributes them over the land where they root and produce new life.

Also in the realm of human relations, I have seen this tension between scattering and centering show itself in the coming together of small groups. At first, the differences of personalities, backgrounds, and interests present a picture of diversity, but soon the forces of mutual attraction begin to work as the members become acquainted. I understand the centering to be the work of love. It is similar to the mutual attraction between molecules that produced more complex forms of life. Love changes the diversity of "you and I" into the unity of "you and I."

To help us deal with the problem of fragmentation, the first requirement is a focused, positive sense of self, in relation to God and others. This will free us to evaluate our resources objectively and enable us to pursue those areas which are of the most interest and are the most fulfilling. And if we feel fulfilled, we are able to give of ourselves to others in spite of the clamoring of fragmentation.

We are often dependent upon others to help us see ourselves and alter our fragmented way of living. Betty, for example, was a hyperactive person involved in all kinds of activity to such an extent that she was unable to organize her affairs and center herself on any interest that would give her structure and direction. She was a loveable person whom people liked but whom they could not trust to keep her promises. A more fragmented person would have been hard to find, having many competing selves within and distracting demands from outside. In middle life, ten years after her divorce, she met and fell in love with a man who was strong and who saw behind her hyperactivity a deeper self that had never been released. Even before they were married she underwent an amazing transformation. She became more calm, centered, and serene. She, herself, eliminated many of the activities that had fragmented her and she chose a few that she pursued earnestly. Love fulfilled her and gave her power to bring order into her chaotic life. This illustration opens the door to the insight that love in any of its aspects has power to focus and unify.

God and the Giving Self

In the second chapter I discussed how imperative it is to keep fear and trust in dialogue with each other in order to increase the meaning of our pilgrimage. I have also introduced the concept of courage as a source of the power to risk the dialogue, to risk leaning into our fears toward trust in spite of every reason not to trust.

Where does this courage come from? Where can I find

it? It has to be a greater courage than I can find in myself or in my world. I have seen human manifestations of it. I saw my mother transformed, during that part of her ninety years that I witnessed, from a shy, timid, self-effacing, self-doubting person to a strong, self-affirming creative person. She manifested a courage that enabled her to accept all the fear and threats that incapacitated her in the first part of her life and move through them to a life of greater sense of self, of possibility, of power of relationship.

That power to affirm life and oneself in spite of all doubt and fear comes from God, but the meaning of that word God needs reexamination.

The first god I knew did not give me courage. He took away whatever courage I had. He was an awful god. As a child I thought of him as a jealous, vengeful god who had it in for little boys who did not behave. Later, I had a sense of him as another, though divine, person who remained disapproving of much that was developing in me during adolescence. He seemed especially "interested" in and disapproving of sex. He was reputed to love only those who went to church and who did not smoke, drink, or swear, and who supported that which the pillars of the church and community thought was right. He was the big EYE who blocked the development of my I. In fact, I was taught in Sunday school that one became a Christian by crossing out the personal pronoun I, thus making a cross. The effect on me of this kind of god was to cause me to deceive and repress! Even when I went to seminary, my theological "education" failed to penetrate this "bastard theology." Like the god it represented, it was unrelated to my own search for God. My god had become an ideal projection and a competitor in the struggle of wills between him and me. There was no love in this relationship either from him to me or from me to him.

Strangely, when I finally freed myself from this god, I found myself, and a power to love. I discovered a real God behind the frightening, judgmental one with which I had grown up—a God of gods who is the source of all life and who has revealed himself in many ways. He has revealed himself in Jesus as the embodiment of his eternal love and being, revealed himself in such a unique way to tell me of the importance of my relationships to others. Jesus was a man of great courage who enabled others to grow in the face of great risk to himself.

From that I take courage and dare to risk opening and giving myself to others. I know that when we are in relationship, we enable each other to grow and to love. With this courage then, not only can I face the distractors and sort out the fragmentations of life, but I can also face the fateful events and find my destiny. I can face the deaths that my risking for myself and others requires of me. I can face criticism and the evidence of my fallibility and mortality. I find myself affirmed in the Eternal Thou in whom we live and move and have our being.

Now I really understand and accept the nature of the relationship of the Divine Being: Love yourself, love your neighbor, and love Being! When I love you, I love Him and myself; when I love myself, I love you and Him, and when I love Him, I love you and myself. This is the source of courage for me to live and give, in spite of my fears, failures, guilt, and death.

I am troubled by the growing prevalence of a literalistic rendering of a simplistic Jesus whose naïvely understood teachings cause young and old to make him less than he is.

Confronted by a technology that is both building and destroying our civilization, overwhelmed by fears and mistrust, increasing numbers of people are running from the power and majesty of the God of love with all that he gives of courage, to erect an idolatrous image of Jesus that fits the small dimensions of their neuroses. The spirit of exclusion, division, competition, judgmentalism is the fruit of this kind of retreat.

George, for example, is a man whose fear prevented him from facing his true self. His little god has no courage to give him because his god is a projection of, and is no bigger than, George's needs. He has turned to a Jesus who "tells" him that he is right, that others are wrong. Clenching his fists and angrily pounding the table, he tells us that the love of Jesus has driven hate and anger from his heart. This "Jesus" he worships is destroying him, his family, his career, and narrowing the boundaries of his world. He has lost touch with the God of gods who gives courage, who confronts, who heals, and lifts up and strengthens the frightened.

When we are open to the Spirit of the Eternal One who is Love, we are made free to love and give ourselves. Our former need to hide and be defensive is replaced with capacities to share and be open to the varied experiences of our pilgrimage as they occur through the years. We may travel together, youth and age, in this common enterprise we call living. We may learn to love giving our ever new selves to one another.

8
Making Growth Choices

How we survive our years is up to us; the becoming of myself is my own self's task. No one will do it for me although there may be many who will help me, as there are many who will hinder me, whether intentionally or unintentionally. As we saw in the first chapter, nature takes care of our growth for twenty years but from then on we are on our own. Our life is at first expanding and increasingly inclusive. Gradually it begins contracting and excluding. This natural change requires that we take over the work of self-expansion, and keep a zest for living. Such heroic effort calls for the courage I mentioned in the last chapter—the courage to enter into and seek life. We usually find what we are looking for. Making growth choices is, therefore, crucial.

I listened to a man recently who is in his middle forties, still attractive, although paunchy and tired looking. Sprawled inertly in his chair he said with a sigh, "I'm getting old, I guess. I find it harder and harder to get going in the morning. I don't have the same energy I used to have. I wish something would happen to turn me on." The chances are good that nothing is going to happen to turn him on. He is locked into an inert, supine style of life. He has lost his sense of freedom to be and to act. His future is being determined by the way he is living his "now." At present, he seems doomed to age negatively.

Freedom to Choose

We have more freedom than we think we have. Even the man who is on his way to be executed has the freedom to decide how he will go: dragged, kicking and screaming; self-pityingly; hostilely or vengefully; or with self-possession and dignity. There is much talk now about the great hardships that people with fixed or low incomes are experiencing as a result of inflation. To be sure the injustices in our social life are many and cruel, and the plight of many people is desperate. A great difference is to be found, however, in the way different people pass through the same experience. Some are embittered and destroyed; others find a way to hold on to a sense of perspective and to exercise initiative, ingenuity, and good humor.

I once knew a woman who was an invalid, the mother of two sons and the wife of an ineffectual man who made a very inadequate living. In spite of illness and poverty, she radiated a gentle life-giving spirit that was like a blessing. It wasn't that she was unrealistic about her health and living conditions. She was aware and felt the limitations, but within them she had the freedom to be a triumphant person.

We have the same freedom in relation to the effects of growing older, whether in our forties or eighties. We can be "never too old" to be alive and interested unless consciousness is taken away. The forty-year-old man who was feeling his age and finding it harder and harder to get going possessed many potential freedoms: the freedom to think differently about himself, to find something to be really interested in, to sit up in his chair and help his body look human and give his organs a chance to operate normally, to ask me something about myself that could possibly activate an interest of his own. Sadly, however, he did not realize that he had those and other freedoms, that he did not need to be a prisoner of the slowing down process of growing older. Without knowing it he had chosen not to choose living and growing. The next step in his collapsing course was to feel sorry for himself, and to justify his condition by the rationalization, "I am growing old." Already he is caught in a deteriorating vicious circle: failure to choose life—fatigue and depression, illness, further contraction of interest, deterioration of mind and body, age and feebleness, senility, and finally, death—without the satisfactions of having lived. He will never know the triumph of having suffered for a purpose, nor the sense of achievement that comes to those who have the freedom to turn suffering into growth. His suffering will have been heedless and needless.

The opposite kind of choosing is illustrated by the man who was informed at the age of fifty-two that he had inoperable cancer that would kill him in six months at the most. At first he was shocked and depressed. "Life seemed to be over for me," he said. But because he was the kind of man who had made growth choices during the earlier part of his life, he recovered from his depression with the realization that he was not dead yet. He began to resume his life, his relations with his wife and children, his work and his community activities. His new attitude was expressed in his words, "It may be short, but I have a future. I must live each day of it to the fullest." Instead of bemoaning that he had so little time, he chose to think in terms of the quality of the time he could create. In the midst of this period with the shadow of death hanging over him, he reported that he had a greater awareness of the joy of living, of the richness of relationship with his wife and children. Gradually he withdrew from his business, although he continued as much responsibility as his waning strength allowed. These were times of discouragement and fear, but each time he drew on the courage of his faith to trust and say: "Today is the first day of my future." He lived longer than was expected and died a fulfilled man even though his years were cut short. In the face of severe and painful limitation he exercised his freedom to choose life in the face of death. This is what Paul Tillich described as the "courage to be" in the face of the threat of non-being.[1]

Contrasting our two examples, we see that the first man with the possibilities of life before him chooses premature and negative aging; the second man, in the face of increasing limitations of time and strength, chooses growth. Each of us has to ask ourselves how much of the freedom to choose that is available to us do we use; and for what: for life or death; for positive or negative aging?

Choosing A Faith to Live By

Our last illustration makes a most important point: The faith we choose to live by is the one that will affect our aging, and the one by which we will die, since aging and dying are a part of life.

We can have at least two kinds of faith. One is the closed

---

[1] Paul Tillich, *The Courage to Be*, (New Haven: Yale University Press, 1952).

system set of beliefs once and for all accepted and within which one lives; the other is an open dynamic set of beliefs with which one lives dialogically as he deals with the issues of his world.

The closed system is not apt to change, nor is the person who lives within that system apt to change. Because the system is closed it is not open! Not open to any influences, even those that might come from God. Perhaps I should say, it is especially closed to God influences because these influences would be most disturbing. And because the person lives within the thick impenetrable walls of rigid belief he "cocoons" himself in relation to the possibilities of change and growth. The God of this kind of system becomes the God whom I want to think he is, the God of whom I approve, who will okay what I like and want, and whose categories for people and events coincide with mine. The living space in this kind of system grows smaller and smaller. Lacking inclusiveness and the experience of repentance and forgiveness, the "believer" becomes rigid, bitter, weary and aged no matter how old.

When I was ordained into the ministry of the Episcopal Church I received a letter from an aunt who belonged to a church of the closed system. She wrote to mourn my death to God because I had joined myself to a church and its ministry that did not hold the true faith. She firmly believed that the only true faith was the one held by her and that all others were under the condemnation of God. Her God apparently was as small as her mind and heart.

The opposite kind of faith is the open dynamic one. The believer in this instance is an inquiring, trusting person whose understanding of God grows. Such a person uses his faith as a basis for risking dialogue with God, man, and human events, as did the Psalmist, Job and others. Such a person trusts God enough to argue with him if he needs to and he is open to anyone who seems to speak any part of what seems to be the truth. His faith is a basis for both a synthesis of meaning and a platform for exploratory action. Such a position is difficult to maintain today because of the confusions, lack of trust, and uncertainties that mark our life. Caught as we are between trust and mistrust, between hope and despair, between love and hate, we often feel that there is no certainty. We can only stand with faith on the ridge between certainty and uncertainty.

Of course, we would like answers but faith does not give answers. It is more apt to raise questions just as Jesus did with his disciples and others. The life of a pilgrim is marked by a movement from question to question in response to the whole range of our life experiences. An open faith was practiced by Abraham who departed for a country he knew not of, by Jesus who followed his course to its bitter and triumphant end, by Luther who challenged the dogmatism and rigidity of a fascist church, by any one of us who by faith risks all to maintain integrity and trust.

The question is: What kind of faith are you trying to live by? One that contains you and keeps you safe, or one that expands you and moves you into the most that your life can be? Have you created a God to serve you; or have you been grasped by the living God with whom you live in a relationship of both fear and trust? The God you make has no power and therefore faith in him can only accelerate your aging. The living God preserves and renews the vitality of soul and body. "And it shall come to pass . . . that I shall pour out my spirit on all flesh; your sons and your daughters shall prophesy, your old men shall dream dreams, and your young men shall see visions" (Joel 2:28).

Negative and Positive Choices

Negative choices are retreat choices unless the retreat is a part of a strategy for advance. The army commander may have to order a retreat in order to recoup for a later advance; we may have to withdraw for the sake of rest and perspective before tackling a crucial task. But negative retreat is an end in itself and leads to a sterile end. What are some negative choices? Surrendering to fear without testing whether you need to; choosing comfort rather than creative tension; choosing thoughtless conformity to what others expect of you. Or, we can become addicted to drugs, TV, gossip, work as an evasion of relationships, and to anything else that robs you of your autonomy. Or, you can build and control a small world by selected attitudes and behaviors; and, by so doing, rob yourself of experiences of ecstasy, and the security of being grounded in something more than yourself that gives meaning to your own existence. Negative choices accelerate aging and cause the juices of one's life to slow down and dry up.

Some of the mechanisms by which we maintain negative choices are well known. The following defense mechanisms retard maturity and accelerate aging:

Rationalization, the process by which we justify ourselves, our ideas and our behavior even though they are destructive.

Displacement occurs when we transfer emotions associated with one person or thing to an unrelated person or object as when we hate an authority because of negative feelings we have toward our fathers.

Conversion occurs when we transfer tension or anxiety or hate or other feelings into a physical symptom, such as headaches, stomachaches, etc.

Projection, attributing to others faults or wishes which are really our own but which are too painful for us to acknowledge.

Idealization, by which we overvalue ourselves or someone we love.

When we overwork these mechanisms—we all use them sometimes—we will inevitably make negative choices and in so doing facilitate negative aging.

Positive choices have the opposite effect and they generate excitement for living and a sense of adventure. When we choose to invest ourselves in something that excites us we become aware of a flow and concentration of energy that is exceptional. Enthusiasm and the openness to being excited! The song of a bird, the heart pulse of a big city, light shining through leaves, sunsets and sunrises, the achievements of human communications in the arts and sciences and in human relationships, the excitement or novelty in something new and also in something old. The excitement that is response to the amazing world outside of us and to the mysterious and wonderful world of our own interior souls.

Choose, therefore, to plunge into life and learn to swim with and against its currents. Choose to say "I am who I am and I look forward to the 'I am' that I am becoming." Choose the acceptance that is there for you to accept that comes from both God and man. Choose to live each day that you are alive with maximum capacity you have for that day. Each day can be an exciting chapter in the whole story of the only life you can have here. I know an artist who is over eighty years old who is always excited at the prospects of each day. She wakens with wonder in anticipation of what she will see, experience and do that day. Though she is wrinkled and shows other signs of age, she has more vitality and enthusiasm than most people many years younger. And her enthusiasm is so infectious that not only does she seem younger than she is, but she makes others feel the same. Banked fires eventually burn themselves out, but fires stoked by interests and creative tasks burn brightly and radiate warmth.

I have stated some general principles for making life promoting choices. I want now to list and discuss some specific choices.

Choose to Be Open

Choose to be open to the voice in you, to your feelings, your intuitions, your thoughts, your insights, your self-evaluations, your fears. Be open to your inner self, the self that is often suppressed and repressed by your own and others' demands. Learn to keep these two selves, your coping self and your inner potential self, in dialogue with each other in order that both may grow and keep your body alive and your spirit responsive.

Be open to the varieties of people, and the experiences you can have with them. One of the sure contributions to negative aging is the drying up of the capacity to enjoy different kinds of people and experiences. When you find yourself not liking or excluding someone reexamine your response. Look for what you may have missed in the situation at first or at second glance. Also ask, What is behind what I don't like that I may find interesting and respond to? One has to work to keep open, because our likes and dislikes become more set with advancing age. Being open does not mean liking everything. We are not born to be sponges. Discriminating openness both feeds and protects us. Openness means accepting without necessarily approving. Behavior in another that we do not approve need not prevent us from accepting the person as one who needs love; but the habit of disapproval without the gift of acceptance makes us lonely people whose vulnerability to negative aging is increased.

Being open will help to keep us flexible and adaptable. A letter from a friend had the following to say about the importance of being open and adaptable: "I find that when I close my mind to people and things, when I refuse to listen to others, when I choose to be with the same people, and decide I am too old to change, I begin to lose both physical and mental energy. One word for all this is rigidity—refusal to risk new things for the sake of staying alive." She continued by stating what she regarded as choices that slowed down deteriorating aging: "I feel more alive when I am open to change and sense in myself an inner resourcefulness; when I work at understanding rather than condemning; and when I listen more and talk less."

Choose to Listen and Love

Following the suggestion in the letter just quoted, choose to listen and love rather than talk and hate. Listening, of course, is a great way to practice openness. And I believe that people who listen are engaging in a tremendous act of love. Attentive listening is a gift of the whole self; heart and mind are fully focused on the other through eyes and ears. Two benefits result from this kind of listening: the one listened to is called forth and enabled to share something of himself; and the one who listens with focused attention is strengthened by making this gift, and enriched by the relationship that true listening creates. For a reminder of how important listening is, refer again to chapter 7.

In contrast, people who are incessant talkers and who thwart response are aggressors and assaulters whose behavior expresses hostility toward the victim, and fear that they might have to listen if the "opponent" managed to get a word in edgewise. The egotism and defensiveness of a verbal bully has a deteriorating effect on his person and diminishes his survival powers. Whereas the listener, by his love, both gives and receives life.

Choose to See Ourselves As We Really Are

This is not always easy to do because from our earliest days we begin to learn defensive ways in which to react to our problems. It takes courage to free our insecurities, fears and anxieties, and be open to the indications that come from others that we are being unreal. There are several realities that we have to face: the inner truth about ourselves which may be painful to face; the truth about others which we may not want to face, accept and deal with; and the truth about the world we live in which at the present time is disturbing because of widely prevalent exploitation and dishonesty in both high and low places. The person who chooses to be real and deal with reality will experience stress, but stress and our constructive response to it can strengthen our powers to cope, grow and age positively.

Choose Goals for Yourself

I think of goals as representing something I want that is worthy of wanting. I offer this suggestion in contrast to living in slavish response to the injunction: "I ought" or "I should."

I am afraid that a majority of church members practice a religion of law and obligation. Being faithful for many means doing what you *ought* to do. I protest that life was not meant to be lived in response to oughts and shoulds. I believe that Jesus made us free of the law so that instead of saying out of obligation or duty, "I *ought* to do so and so," we can say out of love, "I *want* to do so and so." A very favorite text of mine is "You owe no man anything but to love one another, for love is the fulfilling of the law." Oughts and shoulds are spawned by the law, but love frees us to want to live a life of love and privilege. The more we live by law, the more we will be driven by a sense of ought and should. When we live out of love our motivations change from obligation to privilege—from *oughting* to *wanting*.

Oughting is dehumanizing. Wanting to give love is humanizing. People who live by the rule book are apt to be judgmental and authoritarian. Even the Bible can be turned into a life-denying rule book. On the contrary, people who care about persons and want to give love in its many varieties are warm, open, and spontaneous, and such is the true intent of Jesus' teachings. People who are ruled by their oughts and shoulds are often rigid in body as well as souls. Their bodies become stiff and unyielding, resulting in stiff necks and back pains, leg cramps and aches that grow out of bodily constrictions. This is because their minds and emotions are constricted. Their sense of obligation and duty create emotional conditions of stress, tightness, and anxiety. Their breathing is shallow, their muscle tone brittle. On the other hand, people who love self, others, and God are able to express wants that are generally beneficial. They're able to take joy in life, to feel and accept pleasure as not only legitimate but desirable. Wanting people—that is, people who want to love, want to give, want to learn, want to be self-disciplined, want to share, want to grow—are people who have pleasure in being who they are and in learning how to act helpfully and constructively.

You say, "Give us some illustrations of wants that are good substitutes for oughts." I will answer by giving you some statements of what I want. I want the freedom of the Spirit which is the promise of the New Testament. Where the Spirit of the Lord is, there is freedom. I want to realize myself—that is, grow myself in the few years in the here and now that I have been given for being Reuel Howe; I want to be aware of and responsive to others—not only my special people, but any who cross my path. I want to explore as much meaning as I can find and assimilate. I want to learn the disciplines that will give me the skills to relate creatively to the natural and human creation. I want to do the work that will build a humane society. I want to be moral without being moralistic. I want to find my unity in Being—God— or whatever name you give the Thou. I want finally to end my days with a happy sigh that I have really lived and feel that others and I are glad that I have lived. I suggest, therefore, that you get out from under the oppression of your oughts and shoulds and learn how to want to love and live with all your being. How great it is to say, "I am doing what I want" and to know that you can't want anything better!

A next step after deciding what you want is to outline the steps by which you plan to achieve your goal. These should be as specific as possible so that you can be easily aware of having worked on an objective at some time during each day. If I want to become a better listener then I will be aware of times when I worked at listening and times when I fell into the old habit of inattention.

Goals on what we want will of course change as we pursue them. The process is one in which we decide what we want; then we work at its accomplishment; next we evaluate what we have done and finally set a new goal. This process would be repeated endlessly, moving from purpose to purpose, experiencing the growth and excitement of creative aging.

Choose Focusing on Resources

I find that most people I work with are preoccupied by problems, weighted down emotionally by them, and paralyzed in their inability to deal with them. And no wonder because they only see the task and not the possible resources for dealing with the problems. The basis of creative thinking and action is being aware that for every problem there are existing resources in oneself, in others, and in the general environment that can be employed to help meet the problem or find a more constructive way to live with it. When I ask members of a group to identify a personal problem, they do so quickly and without difficulty. It is usually a matter of choosing one among many. But when I ask them to identify a personal resource, such as imagination, ingenuity, or the ability to act positively in relation to a negative situation, they falter, are slow to get a resource in focus, and are usually embarrassed to report it because it seems immodest. All of which reveals how problem-centered we are, and how blind we are to resources that are ours to use. It is no wonder that so many people have such a low sense of self-esteem.

I learned from my mother when I was fifteen how creativity can bring hope out of tragedy and the power of recovery in the midst of falling.

After a devastating fire that wiped us out, except for the clothes on our backs, my father and I were returning with supplies through the woods from a distant village and found that my mother had arranged a lunch on a log in the middle of which she had set a rusty tin can filled with wild flowers.

That symbolized her capacity to find resources in the midst of heartbreak. And how that heroic use of so little lifted our hearts! That act symbolizes her story, and it became mine; and with it I participate in Jesus' story. In the midst of sadness and loss there is to be found joy; in the midst of tragedy, hope. This way of living kept her alive into her ninetieth year.

Do you have any wild flowers in a rusty tin can not far from your smoking ruins?

Choose a Renewing Source Outside of Yourself

The busier one is, the harder it is to keep a perspective and to maintain courage for frontier living and overcome the disillusionments and other threats that come out of committed living. The times call for serenity in the midst of chaos, the courage to risk the unknown and the determination to decide and act in the face of change.

I cannot pull all of this out of myself. I must choose to open myself to all manifestations of God and let him address me by whatever means. For years I hammered at the door of heaven trying to force myself on the attention of Being itself. From Jesus himself I finally learned that I am accepted, that I do not have to strive to be known and to have my purposes served. I needed only to accept the acceptance of love, and allow the presence of the Eternal Thou to enter into my Thou and the Thou of others. Therefore, I wait and let the Lord speak, however he will, with the hope that I will have the eyes to see, the ears to hear, and the heart and mind to respond. It is such a wonderful relief to know that I do not have to direct God, I have only to respond; that I do not have to direct others, but only respond and trust the dialogue of the I and Thou. The wear and tear is lessened, the renewal is increased, and life takes on new excitement!

Learn to Let Go

In the context of the kind of trust I have just described we can choose to learn how to let go and how to compensate. As we grow older we are faced with losses, sufferings, failures, and deaths. All of these cause in us feelings of bereavement, that is, sorrow for what we have lost or for what has been taken from us. Some experience these losses bitterly, and never recover from them; others are able to relinquish what is gone with an acceptance of the loss and a treasuring of the meaning of what had been a cherished part of their lives. These latter persons are able to find compensations which they pursue with interest and hope.

Such attitudes and behavior are responses to the death-life, death-life rhythm that I discussed in Chapter 2. There we saw that it is the rhythm of growth whether we are on the ascending scale of increasing powers, or on the descending scale of decreasing powers. The principle of relinquishment as a way of releasing ourselves from the bondage of fixation dependence in order to grow is true during all the cycles of our life. We are told that when we fall down we should relax. Learning to relinquish what we are losing is a way of relaxing. Acceptance of the rhythm of life—of gain and loss, bereavement and hope, of deprivation and compensation—frees us from the suction of fear and releases us to respond to trust. We thus experience the triumphant rhythm of fear and trust.

We can learn to live this rhythm of relinquishment and compensation, of fear and trust in the earlier years of our lives so that when we reach the later years when their power will be more greatly needed we will have it. I have just been through this kind of experience and I share it not to boast or to set myself up as an example, but as an illustration of what I mean.

I have just relinquished the directorship of the Institute for Advanced Pastoral Studies that I, with others, founded in 1957. That experiment in continuing theological education succeeded far beyond all my dreams for it. The past seventeen years were the part of my professional career for which all that went before was preparation. It was my "baby" and much of the meaning of my life depended on it. I had wondered how I would respond when the time came when I would have to turn it over to others; and, quite frankly, many of my friends wondered if I could. The time came for resignation. I am thankful that I am relinquishing with a minimum of distress even while continuing on the scene as a part-time member of the staff. I am able to do it because of repeated relinquishments that I have made during my life. In my twenties I was helped to let go of health in order to regain it on an adjusted basis. I have also learned to let go of illusions about myself in order to accept the realism of who and what I am; to let go of illusions about others and find the truth about them and learn to live responsively to that truth. It has been necessary to let go of hopes for achievement that were never realized and to turn the disappointments into renewed determination. Miscellaneous loves have to be surrendered for the sake of true and enduring love. Cherished ideas and beliefs that were either wrong or outgrown had to be given up for the sake of ideas and beliefs that painfully expanded my comprehension of truth. How hard it is to let go of friends who for one reason or another are no longer friends; to let go of privileges; to let go of justice as an expectation in this life; to let go of loved ones and learn to live alone until the final death reunites us all. All of these and other experiences of surrender I now see have strengthened me for the latter years of my life with an enthusiasm for what yet may be but also with a readiness for the final relinquishments.

This chapter has been about choosing—choosing growth choices. When we think about choices we are driven to deciding what we really want. I have asked myself that question. My answer is: I want to have lived so that when I come to my end I want to be glad, and I want others to be glad that I have lived. What do you want? Try to decide when you are younger what you really want! It will be a big step toward learning to love living.

9
Learning for "Now" and "Then"

A woman in her middle forties was disturbed by an awareness of how fast the years were passing and how old she was becoming. She said to a friend who was considerably older: "I wish I could grow old gracefully, like you."

"My dear," the second woman replied, "You don't grow old. When you cease to grow, you *are* old."

Apathetic and senile older people have lost their powers and capacities to be alive not because they are old but because they have lost their interests and have nothing to do that stimulates their minds and hearts. When they become useless to themselves and society they degenerate into a vegetable-like condition with nothing to look forward to but a lonely life and death. If their interests could be rearoused their condition would improve at least somewhat. Better still, the loss of interest and capacity could be prevented. And that is what this chapter is all about.

Need of Education for the Whole Life

How unfortunate it is that our education, as received from conventional schools and churches, does not more adequately provide a comprehensive grounding for the development of a philosophy and way of life that prepares us not only for our technical responsibilities but for the formulation of values and lifelong interests. Most of our education is aimed at the needs of children, adolescents, and younger adults who are maturing physically and psychologically and getting established in their jobs and careers. Education of the emotions is largely neglected and so also are the interior needs of the human soul. We need a continuing education that also gives a basic philosophy for living the maturer and older years; an education that would equip us when our children are grown; when our occupational ceiling is known or suspected; and when we have to look elsewhere than to our work for soul satisfactions. We need an education that prepares older people for finding joy and fulfillment in the ultimate prize of old age—the growth of wisdom. In Job 12:12 we read, "Wisdom is with the aged, and understanding in length of days."

Educated people are often "illiterates." Lawyers, engineers, clergy, teachers, business leaders, industrialists, for the most part, are supposed to be educated people. They can read and write, they have mastered the skills of their work, and can innovate to some degree within the limits of their specialty, but many of them are lacking in interest and knowledge in other fields, and they cannot think creatively nor respond imaginatively to challenges in new situations of living. They are not building broadening interests, expanding the areas of their knowledge, engaging in reflective thinking, and therefore, growing in wisdom. Such deficiencies are a personal loss to them and an equal loss to our culture. The final result is the impoverishment of the middle and final years of a person's life. Emptiness of life drains vitality. What is needed is a continuing purpose, a consistent testing and feedback from others as to whether we are growing, and a will to love and live. These ways of living can be developed each year.

Two Examples

Gary, for example, is a man who failed to plan for the changes that would inevitably occur during his life. His goal was to become a school administrator. To this end he devoted all his study and activities. Most of his traveling was to professional meetings. His friends were people in the same field and when they met they talked shop. He was successful and lived a full life occupationally. He loved his family but his devotion to them was subordinate to his devotion to his career. When he retired at sixty-five the major interest that tied him to the meaning of his life was severed. Suddenly, there was nothing for him to do, he could not work at his interests, he had no other activities, and, most tragically of all, he had no sustaining philosophy that could form a basis for a creative approach to his changed life situation. He had depended on his work for the maintenance of his sense of self and when that was taken away he was bankrupt and bereft. Now he is restless, fretful, lost, and does not know what to do with himself. He had not prepared for this time in his life.

Fred, on the other hand, was prepared. When retirement came he had developed a wide range of interests, volunteered for several community services and in a few months found himself employed part time by a government agency working in an area that was related to his lifetime occupation. He is happy and fulfilled because he is still actively engaged in his pilgrimage.

The difference between these two men is to be found in the thinking, planning, and equipping of themselves as resourceful people. Gary stopped growing and is old. Fred is still growing and, while accumulating years, may never become old.

Laying Foundations for Youthful Aging

The time to begin laying these foundations should be no later than the middle and late thirties and early forties. We begin life as egocentric children. Satisfaction of our needs is imperative to our survival. When we cry someone rushes to care for us and naturally we begin to experience ourselves as the center of the universe, a condition from which we will struggle to recover for the rest of our lives. So in the very earliest years of our pilgrimage our experience of being loved and cared for also builds in us an illusion that all life revolves around us. Later experiences seek to disillusion us in order that we may find our real place in the order of persons and things; that is, one important person among many.

Education and training of the child and youth are to equip him for his pilgrimage from birth to life and he must acquire knowledge, skill, and maturity for the processes, tasks and relationships in which he will be involved.

Later youth and young adulthood are concerned with finding and employing themselves, making their mark, in "matching" and "hatching." That is, establishing families. This preoccupation can make for a very small world of ourselves, our families and our work. Acquisition and getting established is the "name of the game," and there is not much left for any other interests. During this period a concern for religion, spiritual values, and relationships often diminishes and may be smothered permanently by preoccupations with establishment of self, marriage, and career. Other pilgrims, however, emerge from their preoccupation and efforts to a realization of deeper values and larger dimensions of being.

Thus in the middle years we may begin to be more aware of the great world beyond our personal, family, and career realms. Hopefully by this age we have achieved some sense of self, some value base for living, and have begun to accumulate raw materials for enriching thought and enlarging relationships. At this age we are faced with the question, "What can we accumulate while we are younger and more active that we can take with us into older years that will increase our resourcefulness as persons?

Find a Center Outside of Self

No one should ever abandon growing a sense of self and a sense of self worth, but our sense of self will grow more surely and naturally as we learn to relate to centers outside of self. A simple manifestation of this growth is that we begin to think about others more and about ourselves less. Having enjoyed self interest in the earlier years we now enjoy interest in others, being aware of their concerns, being more able to relate to them without competition and with more tolerance and with less need to be judgmental where they differ from us. This switch from predominantly self interest to predominantly other interest makes for a more mature and joyous person, and is indispensable if we are to prevent the destructive self preoccupations of older people who have aged negatively. They have aged negatively because they are not securely tied to a center outside of themselves.

The core point of Jesus' teaching is pertinent here. He

said: "Love the Lord God, and your neighbor as yourself." His instruction is simple and clear, but hard for us to accept because we have distorted it. He said:"Love yourself." Unless I love myself, I cannot love you; if I love not myself and fail to hold myself in good esteem I have nothing with which to be humble and reverent. Then he amplifies: "Love your neighbor as yourself." Here we see how he wants our love to move out to include others and give them the reverence and care that each person merits just because he or she exists. This is not easy and therefore calls for the full power of love. The neighbor and the world of the neighbor with all of its complexities, structures, tensions, contradictions, achievements, failures are our focus for loving attention and response. To the degree we give ourselves to others our own selves will be purified and strengthened. Finally, to truly love myself and my neighbor is to love God who is the source of all being. It is presumptuous to say what God wants, but I presume to suggest that God wants to be loved by the way we live with ourselves and others and the world he created.

Thus the movement from love of self, to love of others, and to love of God represents the movement from ourself as a center to centers outside of ourselves. Such love that moves out to concerns outside of self dispels fear and prevents the stagnating effects of aging where persons are preoccupied and worried about themselves to the exclusion of everything else. Bertrand Russell, English philosopher, said in his late eighties: "It is best to make your interests gradually wider and more impersonal until bit by bit the walls of the ego recede, and your life becomes increasingly merged in the universal life." Awareness means that the meanings of one's own life more and more merge with those of men of all ages.

Cultivate Passions

Instead of "passions" I could have written "sustaining enthusiasms." But passion is a powerful word. When I give myself passionately I give myself wholly, fully focused on something or someone outside of myself and experience a power of being that is exciting.

The passion of love, for instance, is self-forgetting, transforming, and energizing. Mind and body are accelerated to feats of concentration and endurance that are phenomenal. The same can be true when we find other objects of passionate devotion. The maintenance of youthfulness and a desire to grow and live depend in part on pursuing something that really interests us and turns us on.

These passionate interests may change from time to time but before one interest passes we should be searching for a new one to take its place to stimulate physical, emotional, and spiritual exertion and achievement. As we move from year to year we can be aware and perhaps keep a list of things that we think we might like to pursue while devoting ourselves to one of them in addition to our job. In this way we can hold a reservoir of potential interests to which we can turn when we need them. When I was passing through my forties and was experiencing a serious crisis in my relationships I designed, planted, and cultivated a garden of 100 rose bushes. I cannot begin to number the benefits of this "passion" that the beautiful roses gave to others and to me. Through the years that I devoted myself to that project I experienced purification, integration, renewed confidence and hope for the future. At other times I turned to sculpture, model railroading, briefly to pottery, refinishing of furniture and, of course, writing. All of these, plus new interests, can be developed and wait only my turning to them as resources for creative and purposeful expression. My awareness of these available areas for enthusiastic activity give me a sense of security for my future. It is great to know that I shall probably never be "unemployed" or lacking in some passionate interest. As I have grown older and approached the senior years I have had the comfort and reassurance of knowing that no matter how old I might become or how little I might be able to do because of infirmities there would always be something to make life interesting and worth living.

There is also the possibility that along with one's occupation, or later after retirement, any one of these special interests might develop into a new career. Many a person's hobby has grown into a career. The maintaining of passionate interests is a powerful resource for continuing a creative pilgrimage from birth to life even to the very edge of the grave.

Learn New Skills

Adult education is one of the largest, most rapidly growing industries and is carried on by colleges, schools, and community organizations of various kinds. Many of these courses are given in the evening as well as the afternoon so working men and women also can make use of them. One way of developing areas of passionate interest is to learn the knowledge and skills necessary for its effective pursuit. As preparation for later and more leisurely years many people elect to take those courses that interest them and equip them with skills for pursuing their vocations and developing avocations for expression. If we procrastinate about learning the skills necessary to do some things that interest us, we will experience only disappointment and frustration. Too many people live lives that are strewn with repeated self-disappointments. As we accumulate these failures we dry up our potential creativity, sap our power to be enthusiastic, increase our self doubt, decrease our sense of worth, rob our bodies of vitality. Positive results are experienced when our dreams turn into realities as we learn the disciplines necessary to fulfill them.

The area of interest in which skills can be learned are: communication, including personal and technological; some area of human relations, such as personal growth, marriage, working with the disadvantaged, personal relationships, etc.; community affairs and action; arts and crafts, hobbies, new forms of exercise especially those suitable to physical changes that accompany growing older. We can try to get in touch with the needs, talents, and interests that are in us and search for the skill that we need to actualize our potential.

Improve Present Relationships

The thirties and forties can be crisis years for family relationships and if these crises are not being met then they will continue to grow and will deteriorate the same relationship in the later years. At the risk of oversimplification, the possibilities for the future of marriage are resentment and frustration with possible separation; or boredom with the development of subtle cruelties expressed toward each other; or growing affection and thankfulness for a tender, sustaining and mutually affirming care of one another. We can also work at improving our relationships with other people; our children, friends, colleagues, neighbors, and the many people we meet along the way.

Some basic attitudes that block improved relationships are: our need to be right about everything rather than be in relation; our need to possess and control others even to the extent of trying to remake them to our liking; our tendency, which may increase with the years, to be suspicious of what they think about us and of what they may be saying about us; our defensiveness that keeps us from seeing how we need to change in order to improve our capacity for mutual relationship; and our failure to communicate, to listen, speak, and deal with the threatening content of our relationships. The more deep-seated that these and other negative responses become the less we are able to grow closer to members of our families and friends.

All of us come into our middle years with certain incapacities for living affectionately and caringly. Some are acquired in childhood and youth which may be accentuated by later behavior; others are acquired later. A great danger in living with others is falling into ruts—attitudinal and behavioral ruts by which we incarcerate ourselves and others in monotony and stereotypes thus stifling the creative potential that exists in all of us for living more spontaneously and responsively. Such rigidities have alienating effects on relationships and suffocating effects on self realization. Among the debilitating ruts is the one in which we fail to recognize the changes, often for the better, that occur in the people we live with. They may change, become more open, more capable of give and take, ready to take risks for the sake of growth, but we continue to relate to them as they used to be. When this happens neither they, nor we, nor our relationships benefit fully from the change that has occurred. Such denials age us negatively and prevent the development of a capacity to give and receive affection and care with consequent benefits of renewal.

If and when it becomes plain to us in our middle years that barriers to relationship are taking serious toll, we may try to do two things. First we—hopefully both the partners—can share an awareness of difficulties and try to help each other deal with them. If it proves too much for us, a third person should be consulted, preferably someone professionally trained and not close to us, to guide us into a more open and responsive kind of communication. Such assistance for our troubled relationships makes as much sense as taking our sick bodies to a physician or our aching teeth to a dentist. Actually we might contemplate the possibility of preventive help for relationships as we do for our bodies, going for a check-up to make sure all functions are "go." In addition to individuals who might help us keep the flow of love and affection going in our relationships, there are various kinds of groups in which meeting with other pilgrims under adequate guidance may help us gain new insight and uncover new resources for living together.

Improvement of relationships is indispensable for the maintenance of vitality and a reason for growing and living.

Span the Gaps

Another source of learning during our advancing years is to keep in touch with people who are different from us in years, race, religion, place of living, and place in society. "Ghettoism" seems to come easily to all of us. I use the term ghettoism to cover all segregation. Rather than ridicule or write others off as being beneath our notice, we need to listen to them and try to find in them that which is like us and vice versa. Then let's study the difference for the sake of what it might teach us.

One of the obvious ghettos is the ghetto of age. Youth, emotionally and culturally, is apt to be isolated from people older than themselves. Elderly people tend to be isolated in the ghetto of age. Parents may be ghettoed from their children and from their own parents. Our contemporary nuclear family situation, contrasted with earlier families that included all ages, require that we make studied efforts to break down the walls of separation. It can be done. We can keep in touch with the ages we have passed through partly by making an effort to remember our own experiences and attitudes when we were a child and a youth and a young adult just starting out; and on the basis of remembering, listen and empathize with those who are following us in their pilgrimage. Also we may, if we will, observe, evaluate, and appreciate those who have preceded us in their pilgrimage. In them we will see what we would like to avoid, and also what encourages us. I have heard younger people express appreciation to older persons for showing them that it is possible to be older and still be youthful in spirit, alert and interested, experienced and tolerant, and filled with wisdom and love of fun. Both younger and older benefit from a reciprocal, dialogical relationship. The first and hardest step for the older person is to want to be with and to learn from younger ones. Once that desire is present many ways will be discovered to bring about intercommunication. The best teachers in educational institutions or churches are people who want to be with people and to mutually share what it means to live their common life. Then the content of the course will come alive no matter what it is.

The same understandings apply equally well to other ghettos where loving and creative people may be unwittingly trapped: racial or ethnic, suburban or inner city, social, teacher-pupil, or religious segregations. The ecumenical movement is a movement to bring all persons into one "house"—to achieve openness to each other and to find the complementary in differences. Briefly, the bigot ages faster and more distressingly than the ecumenical dialogical person who grows older with charity and grace.

Keep Abreast of World Events

As we have seen, one of the dangers in growing older is allowing the sphere of our interest to narrow even to the point of only being interested in what is happening to our bodies: our temperature, our pulse, our digestion, our pains. That small world, in whatever condition, will be better if its occupant has outside interests. We need, therefore, to keep up with the news of world affairs and of local community events. This can be done by listening to the news and quality presentations on TV, and by resisting the temptation to succumb to the mindless programs, and the inanities of some TV advertising which persistently draws our attention back to interests centering in the condition of our bodies.

Subscribe to papers, magazines, and journals that provide intelligent reporting of news and developments in the fields of research and exploration. Read editorial opinion critically and try not to allow ourselves to be uncritical slaves to the opinions of any one writer. Hold on to our independent judgment and resist the suction of popular opinion that seeks to draw us into a vortex of mindless conformity. We need also to resist the temptation to be disgusted with human events. Have sympathy for the human plight: out of our ingenuity man has created some things more complex than we can operate, while, emotionally, being only lately out of the jungle.

We also will want to be as active as possible in determining world and community events by voting, by wiring and writing to congressmen (very few people do it as compared to the number of people who might); by supporting and belonging to citizens' lobbies that multiply the power of the private citizen to combat vested interest lobbies, partisan tendencies of legislators and the inertia and dishonesty of some of our representatives and public officials. We can also volunteer for special services such as making telephone calls, attending public opinion meetings, offering ourselves in the interest of human welfare. Every activity is a way of keeping the mind alert, emotions responsive and persons related to the mainstream of life. No matter how old we are—forty, sixty, eighty —we need for our own sakes to be in the arena of human effort. The world needs every creative voice and hand it can get.

Broaden Your Reading

In addition to participating in current events we can grow and keep alive by living vicariously through reading all kinds of books. I have a friend who makes a weekly trip to the library where he looks over the new books on display and chooses and reserves a wide selection for reading when the books are released for circulation. He chooses books about fields that are strange as well as some that are familiar to him. He reads books in some fields very carefully; others he thumbs through more hastily, but sufficiently, to familiarize himself with possible interests that might be germinated.

While waiting in my doctor's office I found that the only magazine left for me to read was *Popular Mechanics,* containing advertising and articles that do not naturally attract me. Turning the pages I found my interest quickened by an article on the creative use of tools even though I am not much of a tool user.

Reading, therefore, is a way of traveling, exploring, and expanding the horizons within which we live. We can move at will into any period of history, into the lives of famous people and the everyday life of their time. As we grow older we are able to identify our own experiences and insights with those of people in all generations. Reading can project us into the future and its possibilities so that the whole panorama of past, present, and future is laid out for our imaginative participation. And there is no art, craft, science, or other human interest that is not open to exploration through the media of word and picture. From it comes also the acquisition of knowledge, the stimulation of imagination, and the sense of perspective for one's own suffering. Reading will help us put the injustices and distortions of our own society in perspective. Through it, too, we explore the majesty of space and the intricacies of the minute forms of life. The wonders of our human powers of creativity are opened to us as well as an awareness of our inability to operate what we create. Through reading we can become acquainted with the varieties and the complementaries of men's thought, their religious responses, and feel kinship with all worshipers.

As we grow older such reading opens our eyes, minds, and hearts to an ever wider world in which potential interest for us is unlimited. All will be material for reflection and the growing of wisdom. More and more there will be a place in our society for the older and wiser persons. The expansion of technology which is the work of youth will reach a time when the dilemmas of machine and process will demand control by heart and wisdom in order to save itself from chaos and calamity. When perspective, tolerance, concern for values, and power to resist greed and temptation are needed to save us from the effect of unrestrained technology and dehumanization, a place will be made for those whose living has grown wisdom. The question is: "Will awareness of such need come before chaos and destruction?"

Learn to Accept Change and to Change

Life and growth produce change; no life and growth can occur without change. Staying alive and growing, therefore, calls for capacities to accept change and to change within ourselves as a normal expectation. All too frequently, however, we begin to fight change and to want things to stay the way they were, even if they were not very good. Reasons for resistance to change are not hard to identify. Fear of change is a primitive fear: it calls for adjustment and adaptation, for learning new ways of responding; and for using our resources about which we always have more or less doubt.

We need to be aware of the dangers of changing just for the sake of change when it is a form of mindless restlessness. Some people love to innovate for the sake of innovation and are suspicious of anything old that comes from tradition. We need to keep a vibrant tension between ancient good and contemporary values. While "time makes ancient good uncouth" there comes out of the past a timeless truth that has meaning for present perplexities and dilemmas. And yet it also is true, "new occasions teach new duties."

Some questions that each of us must ask in each period of our lives are: Have we changed our ideas lately on at least one major issue? Have we considered the possible obsolescence of views now held? Do we seek for improved understanding of ourselves, of others and of our situations? Have our convictions grown and become more inclusive? How flexible are our feelings? How stubbornly negative are they? How openly positive are they? Our answers to these questions will influence how we age: dogmatically and bitterly; or inclusively and growingly.

Love learning and enjoy its fruits through the whole of your life until you draw your last breath.

10

It's Not Too Late—
Love Being Older

I invite young people to pay particular attention to this chapter. Do not be tempted to skip over it because your own aging seems such a distant problem. Instead, consider that now is the right time to start growing into the person you want to be then. Furthermore, now, while you are young and actively engaged in personal and community planning, is the right time to create your own future environment. The more you can do to encourage and include today's older generations, the more pleasant and productive tomorrow will be for you.

Writer Booth Tarkington was younger in his seventies than many men in their thirties. Once, when he was seventy-five he was asked whether old people felt old in spirit. He replied, "I don't know. Why don't you ask someone who is old?"

All who live accumulate years. How old we grow depends in part upon us. Each person to some degree has a choice between what I have called negative or positive aging. Negative aging is aging without having lived, without fulfillment, accompanied by feelings of fear and resentment. Positive aging is a continuation of adventuresome living, a pursuit of a sense of purpose, and an increasing awareness that one's life is being fulfilled in spite of frustrations, deprivations, and the sure approach of death. The foundations of positive aging are laid in the earlier years, long before aging is a concern. A younger person, for example, who learns that the meanings of failure can be recycled into insight for growth has begun a style of life that will renew him as he moves from year to year. Instead of allowing himself to be defeated, he will wrest some triumphs and satisfactions from what may have been a bruising struggle.

None of us is going to get out of this world alive. It would seem, therefore, to make sense that we learn how to live in it as long and as well as we can. Our insurance against tomorrow is what we do today. Your today may be a day in your thirty-fifth year; mine may be in my sixty-eighth—it matters not. Why does one man, born the same day as another, grow older so much faster? Which one are you? And which one do you want to be?

The kind of older person we become will be influenced by the way we live today. Even though we may have lived yesterday in a way that we regret and may wish we had lived more thoughtfully, we still have a choice in our older years. We can choose to look for clouds or for sunshine. We can choose to look for slights, disappointments, frustrations, deprivations and thus make ourselves feel worse and age faster. Or, we can look for what we can give, even a smile. We can expect times of fulfillment and joys; we can find compensations for deprivations. A man who had to give up tennis after a lifetime of vigorous playing, found joy and benefit in yoga. Yesterday it was tennis; today it is yoga—both give him pleasure and keep his body and soul living harmoniously together.

Retrospection vs. Reminiscing

And how does an older person live with his past, resentfully or retrospectively? Recently, I viewed a retrospective exhibit of an artist. It occurred to me again, as it had several times before, that my life is like a gallery of paintings. I have often walked through its halls and rooms and viewed again and again the paintings of my life. Some of them are dim with age, others bright with the colors more recently applied. Some of the pictures are portraits, others depict scenes, and still others are action pictures representing events. Many moods are represented: peaceful, joyful, painful, embarrassing, reassuring, inspiring, bloody, and above all, revealing. As I walk among them, stopping here and there at different times, I gain perspective on my life, sense its drama, discover its continuity. It represents many different aspects of my pilgrimage, its peaks and depressions, its successes and failures. I have come to see that through each picture shines the essential character of myself, in spite of and because of all the changes and confusions encountered along the way. It is good to know that there is continuity of self from six to sixty. It is good to see in the "paintings" my capacity to live, grow, and learn in the midst of failure, neurosis, ill fortune, and internal and external demonic forces. So I visit my gallery often to reflect and keep in touch with the still unfolding meanings of my story.

This exercise is different from reminiscing, which so easily becomes a monstrous dwelling on the past without critical appraisal. Elderly people are prone to this sort of thing in the process of which memories become distorted, retelling becomes obsessive, and listeners become bored. Retrospection, on the other hand, can become a study of the past for the sake of the active continuation of my life.

Older people, as well as younger people, can live the present day for its own sake, and as preparation for the next day and the future.

I have known creative older people who have retained a sense of excitement for each day and its possibilities. "Being interested and not being bored is my responsibility," said one elderly person. Needless to say, she did not acquire the talent to be interested after she reached advanced years. She built this way of living as she moved from year to year.

Thus, one learns to love being old by living each day on the way with enthusiasm, by keeping in touch with one's unfolding story, and by letting tomorrow care for itself. To make old age a success, we must start while we are young.

Junking Incorrect Beliefs About Aging

Is there any reasonable basis for the hopefulness about being older as expressed in this book, and particularly in the above paragraphs? Obviously, I believe there is.

We can be encouraged by a number of scientific studies which are exposing incorrect beliefs about aging. Many people worry that as they grow older their memories will become dim or they will not be able to think as quickly as they could when they were younger. At a wedding reception recently an older gentleman apologized for not being able to remember the names of people he knew. He said, "Now that I am old, my memory is not as good as it used to be." I asked him if he had had difficulty remembering names when he was younger. The question startled him and after a moment he laughed and said, "Come to think of it, I did."

Recent studies have shown that rather than a loss of mental alertness there are other factors involved.

For example, one study points out that because old age is usually pictured as bringing memory loss, many older people come to expect it and therefore exaggerate and worry about every lapse. Everyone, at every age, may have trouble remembering something at one time or another. But as we grow older, these instances, which we ignored during our younger years, take on a new importance. This can make us anxious and actually create difficulty where none existed. Tests show that older people, when not pressured by time, do just as well as younger ones on memory tests. Once again, the only problem is that older people, anxious about their memories, may become more nervous under pressure, do less well and, thus, feed their anxiety. Loss of memory is not a necessary condition. The myth that one loses memory when old causes the problem.

Depression and Memory Loss

There is a condition, however, that can cause a failing memory, but, again, the cause is not mental but emotional. Many older people who experience memory loss assume that it reflects the onset and progression of senility. But in an exciting and hopeful development, it can now be reported that in some instances memory can be restored by alleviating depression.

Drs. R. J. Shider and Carl Salzman, members of the faculty at the Harvard Medical School and clinical and research psychiatrists at Massachusetts Mental Health Center, have been studying depression and forgetfulness in the elderly for the past three years.

"When depression strikes elderly individuals, it is commonly a response to stressful situations which have arisen in their lives. Not uncommonly, their close friends and relatives are dying, often causing severe emotional strain. Some persons fall victim to depression as they contemplate how relatively little time they have left to live, and how much they want to accomplish in that limited amount of time. Still others face the realization that they are not going to accomplish the high goals they set for themselves in life. Their careers have not turned out as planned. Such individuals may feel a sense of frustration, defeat and lack of self-worth, and may succumb to depression." [1]

How adaptable elderly people are to deprivations and changes in their later years depends in part on how well they have trained themselves in earlier years. My guess is that most older individuals have drifted into age without thought, plan, or purpose and are therefore unprepared victims of what their life experiences have done and are doing to them. A natural consequence of an empty entrance into age would be depression, and certainly many older people show that their emotional level is on the depressed side. Left to themselves they have few flexible alternatives and less natural forces at their disposal to help fight the onset of depression as a response to a severe disappointment.

On the other hand, the prepared older person, the one who has lived his life in ways that give him strength and resources for this later stage of his pilgrimage, will be less prone to depressive responses and to distressing events. The pilgrim, for example, who has repeatedly passed through the death-life, death-life rhythms of living will have acquired a point of view and resources for the requirements of his pres-

---

[1] Jay Winsten, *"A Way to Reverse Memory Loss,"* Harvard Medical School.

ent stage of life. He will not have to withdraw into himself and also withdraw his investment in people, things, and experiences.

When withdrawal becomes a way of life, as we saw in chapter 2, and people become afraid to risk loss and growth they begin to die both literally and figuratively. Their minds and emotions lose their power to function. Some of the symptoms of this death are moodiness, fear, irritability, preoccupation with the past, loss of motor power, and loss of memory for present events. The picture becomes one of senility. But this kind of senility is to be found in thirty-year-olds as well as the elderly.

Senility is not a necessary condition. I want, instead, to affirm a fact: people who have aged unhappily and surrendered to weakness and emptiness can change if they want. They can find other interests and other ways to get attention than preoccupation with bodily disfunctions and complaints.

In chapter 2 I mentioned an elderly gentleman, Mr. C., who expressed concern that the diagram I was using made clear to him that he had withdrawn from real living. Further conversation revealed that he had retired from a self-employed position, largely at the request of his wife. His health was good at the age of seventy. Mr. C. had enjoyed his work and association with all kinds of people. Mrs. C, however, was looking forward to a more relaxed way of life that his retirement would permit. He had expected to travel, acquire new interests, and spend more time with his family and intimate friends. He had never taken time to develop hobbies.

After he retired Mr. C. became bored, resentful, frustrated, and irritable. He discovered that his mental capacities were suddenly failing. Because he had lost a sense of purpose his habits of cleanliness and dress began to deteriorate. He was most distressed that he had suffered a loss of memory. Conversation with him and Mrs. C. revealed that their communication with each other had broken down.

Further conversations made possible an evaluation of what had happened to them. Both were in excellent basic physical condition; their symptoms were a result of emotional stress. The decision to retire was made because she thought he was of an age when he ought to retire. The decision was made abruptly and without much planning. He experienced a sense of bereavement and depression when his work life was suddenly terminated. Even his pleasant and adequate house was too small for him—for her, too, when he was in it all the time—and he did not know what to do with himself. After a period of counseling they remade their decision and began to plan a way of life that restored more enduring interests and activities that served a sustainable purpose. During the course of the counseling they were able to resume their communication with each other, they expressed their anger and resentments and once again learned to enjoy sharing problems with less defensiveness. He found part time employment that engaged his interests and employed his mental powers. His appearance improved, his mental powers were restored, and his enthusiasms for living were rekindled.

Such transformations are possible for the elderly as well as for the younger. Once when I was visiting in the home of a retired president of an industry I saw a miraculous transformation occur. During the early part of my visit Mr. F. was disgruntled and despairing; he sat limply and lifelessly in his chair. The phone rang at his side. He picked it up and listened. Suddenly his face was transformed into a bright smile and he sat up straight in his chair and talked animatedly. All I could tell was that he was hearing good news. After he put the phone down, I learned that a strike in the plant that he had managed for years was almost settled and that both management and labor representatives wanted him to attend a meeting the next day where it was felt that his experience would be of value. The man who put the phone down after that call was a vastly different man from the one who had picked it up a few minutes earlier.

Senility Not Natural

Senility is not natural—it is a disease. Senility is an invention of modern western society and is one of the most damaging self-fulfilling prophesies ever devised. And it can be reduced if not eliminated by reducing the fear of it.

There is, however, some question as to the cause of the disease. Traditionally the main cause of senility has been thought to be arteriosclerosis, hardening of the arteries. This heavily hereditary ailment affects nearly everyone to some degree, clogging the blood vessels with calcium and cholesterol. But autopsies fail to show any constant relation between arteriosclerosis and senility. Brain disease is another cause of senility, due perhaps to some kind of latent virus. Other possible causes of senility include exposure to radiation, early nutritional deprivation, isolation, bereavement, and alcoholism. But Muriel Oberleder, assistant professor of psychiatry at Albert Einstein College of Medicine, says, "Frankly, I believe the people bring senility upon themselves." [2] Dr. James Folsom of the Veteran's Administration agrees: "I think some people have been born senile. They never had an original thought. They don't grab life; they let life grab them." [3] Even if researchers are uncertain about the cause and cure for senility, we have everything to gain by living in ways that will

---

[2] Douglas S. Lorney, *"Senility Is Also a State of Mind," The National Observer,* March 1973.

[3] Ibid.

150

help prevent it. These ways have been suggested in chapters 8 and 9: "Making Growth Choices" and "Learning for Now and Then." In short, the most effective means for reducing the fear of senility is to prepare people for flexible, positive, purposeful living while aging.

Continued Growth for Older People Substantiated

There are other reassuring studies about the continuing capacities of older people. Writing in the March, 1974, issue of *Psychology Today,* Paul B. Baltes and K. Warner Schaie report that in their opinion "general intellectual decline in old age is a myth . . . . Our findings challenge the stereotyped view, and promote a more optimistic one. We have discovered that the old man's boast, 'I'm just as good as I ever was,' may be true, after all." They wrote their article under the title: The Myth of the Twilight Years.

Earlier researchers gained the impression that as far as intelligence is concerned, what goes up must come down. When investigators studied intelligence of people of different ages in a cross-sectional way they were led to believe "that intelligence increases up to early adulthood, reaches a plateau that lasts for about ten years, and begins to decline in a regular fashion around the fourth decade of life."

This view began to change when longitudinal studies were made of a single group of individuals extending sometimes over many years with examination of performance at different ages. These studies indicated that intelligence during maturity and old age did not decline as early as people had originally assumed. As tests improved researchers were able to recognize that on vocabulary and other skills reflecting educational experience, individuals seemed to maintain their adult level of functioning into the sixtieth and seventieth decades or even later years.

In 1956 Drs. Baltes and Schaie launched a major study of five hundred subjects, ranging in age from twenty-one to seventy; and seven years later they retested 301 of the subjects with the same tests. They reported that when they looked at the "results longitudinally comparing a given age group's performance in 1956 with its performance in 1963, they found a decline in only one of the four measures"; namely, the one that tests a person's "ability to shift from familiar to unfamiliar patterns in tasks requiring coordination between visual and motor abilities." [4] There was "no strong age-related change in the ability to shift from one way of thinking to another, within the context of familiar intellectual operations." There was also a systematic increase in the ability of older people to employ the "skills a person acquires through education and acculturation, such as verbal comprehension, numerical skills, and inductive reasoning." The same was true for the ability to "organize and process visual materials such as identifying a picture that was incomplete."

Common sense is a necessary ingredient in this business of staying younger while growing older. There are those older people who try to stay young, hiding from what is happening to them by covering up the signs of age by behavior, by style of dress and by cosmetic alteration. They are unwilling to accept the limitations and renunciations demanded by increasing age. Their efforts are doomed to fail. The more creative alternative that this book is about is based on the distinction between the independence of psychological and spiritual age and biological age. Because of this distinction it is possible for us to disassociate ourselves from our biological age. Instead of following the descending curve of the biological condition, we can redirect ourselves along a horizontal,

---

[4] Paul B. Baltes and K. Warner Schaie, "The Myth of the Twilight Years," *Psychology Today,* March, 1974, p. 35.

even an ascending course. Biologically we may be descending but psychologically and spiritually we can be ascending. The self of such persons is always engaged in the process discussed in chapter 7 of disidentifying and reidentifying the self with the changing conditions of his life.

I can understand from my own struggle how easy it would be to be dragged down by the changes caused by advancing years. How easy it would be to exaggerate the importance of physical ailments and limitations; to allow a narrowing of my fields of interest; to withdraw defensively from change and challenge. Instead I find great advantages in being older. I feel liberated from former tendencies and activities. Conflicts do not occur as frequently, because I am finding other and better ways of dealing with forces and persons that earlier would have caused conflict. There is a broadening of passion into affection and vision, and a maturing of experience that becomes distilled into wisdom. I am grateful for a sense of learning, balance, and serenity, which are a source of profound but quiet joy.

The gaining of one's spiritual self gives independence over internal and external conditions. Such conditions are not ignored. Instead, we learn to live with them as part of our pilgrimage, accept the tasks that face us each day, in the context of our awareness of a freedom to be. I am an older person, but I am more. I am my own self who has survived many relationships, crises, deprivations, and triumphs. My whole pilgrimage from birth to life is preparation, through repeated experiences of living and dying, for the final crisis: the inevitability of death, which incidentally faces us each moment of our life. Some face advanced age and death with fear, anguish, or rebellion proportionate to their attachment to physical life, or their identification of the personality with its physical ties, activities and functions.

But there is a better way; one that can be learned early and, therefore, practiced more easily when we are old.

The life-long cultivation of a free self—even a cultivation in later years of the self that can be free gives us the power to transcend and grow until either destructive disease or death takes control from us. Until then we can direct our psychological and spiritual ascendency. But even those who are suffering the rigors of disease can still shine as luminous selves who prefigure the resurrection.

We older people, and those who will succeed us in each generation, can keep alive in ourselves creative dispositions: dispositions to learn, to associate with people younger than ourselves; dispositions for enjoying differences; for loving; for retrospection and anticipation; for quietness and reflection; for a sense of the ever unfinished continuity of life.

Finally, our living through the successive stages of our life, can be stimulated and promoted by means of assimilation of inspiring models. For example, Michelangelo when he was eighty met a friend in front of St. Peter's in Rome who asked him, "Where are you going?" "I am going to learn," was his reply. *Time* magazine in a recent article on William O. Douglas commented that his eyes were as blue and keen and alert as they were when he was younger. "So, too, is [his] intellect."

We turn now to some other models who, though not as famous, are as extraordinary.

Some Models of Creative Aging

We know of many famous people who continue growingly and creatively into their advanced years. Goethe retained his youthfulness to the end of his life and at eighty-four fell in love with a girl of twenty for whom he wrote one of his finest poems. Golda Meir in her mid-seventies was a leader of her country at a time of national and international conflict working twenty-hour days. There is also Thomas Hart Benton who after a paralyzing stroke at the age of seventy-seven painted a great mural. But we are tempted to think that because these and others we might mention are famous people, they are endowed with exceptional powers. Not so! Here are some others, private citizens, who quietly exhibit the heroism of staying creatively alive.

James G. Driscoll, writing in a recent issue of *The National Observer,* reported on a study done by Jean Wylder and Randy Bolton at the University of Iowa School of Social Work, that showed how the "far side of seventy can glow with controlled fire, striking creativity, and relaxed humor." The stories of these older people are packed with the wisdom of those who have stayed young by staying useful.

One is Edna Wilson, ninety-seven, who began her acting career in TV commercials at the age of ninety. Also Joseph Kolovic, eighty-four, a bookbinder who keeps his catcher's mitt handy for a quick game of catch. Art Myhre, seventy-one, of Cedar Rapids, wanted to paint after retirement, but a stroke left him blind six years ago. Surgery restored part of his sight, and he is back at his easel. Art is also something of a common sense philosopher:

> People who are not old may wonder how a person feels after he has lived three score years and ten . . . We are supposed to have reached the point of no return.
> But my attitude toward this is that I am not willing to accept passivity. I cannot sit and do nothing. There are many things I want to do in this world before I die, and I am not going to let age . . . hinder my doing them . . .
> Time does not hang heavy on my hands. The days go entirely too fast. I like to play golf, I like to tour, I like to visit my children and grandchildren.

Art then adds why life after seventy is so exciting for him:

"You're not tied down, you have no responsibilities, you can do what you want to do, and the result is that I am just as happy and probably more so than I ever was in my life."

Mr. Driscoll continues by telling about James B. Tracy, seventy-four, "a retired engineer of Muscatine, was born in 1899 and hopes to reach 101 so he will have lived in three centuries. 'I have been having a ball in the six years since I retired,' he says. He's been active in organizations supporting the United Nations. He considers himself a world citizen and hopes for 'a period of peace in the world,' though he doesn't expect that to happen even if he lives to be 101. 'But I'm gonna die trying to achieve it,' he declared.

"Cecile Casper of Davenport won't tell her age, and for good reason. 'Not too long ago I was denied a job because I honestly told my age,' she says. She's overcome poverty and racial discrimination in her more than seven decades, so she's not about to let age stop her. She takes care of two nieces, plans to resume dancing lessons, and asserts that if you keep active, 'you don't have to grow old.' "

Photographer Imogen Cunningham picked up her first camera in 1901 and has been taking pictures ever since. Now ninety years old, she is preparing a show of her current works in San Francisco. When asked what was her favorite picture in seventy-two years, she replied, "Hopefully, the one I'll take tomorrow."

Mrs. Frieda Moniak's eightieth birthday was celebrated with a cake and a big jug of wine at Wayne State University in Detroit. She started taking classes in 1959 and is one of the oldest students in the University Center for Adult Education. She holds the record for the highest number of classes, 68, taken in the program. She plans to keep on enrolling to expand her "knowledge of the world."

A friend, Mrs. Betty Burroughs Woodhouse, who is well into her seventies, continues with energy and enthusiasm her career as sculptress, completing commissions in rapid succession. Mother of a large family of children and grandchildren, she happily shares in their activities and expeditions. Before she visited Greece a few years ago, she subscribed to Greek newspapers and magazines and learned both to read and speak modern Greek. Among other activities she goes for long swims in the cold Atlantic that fronts her studio-home. She greets each new day with excitement and a sense of wonder.

These and hundreds of thousands of other older people witness to the indisputable fact that psychological and spiritual powers are able to keep the human spirit alive and growing. They are the heroes in our anti-age society who are beating back the antiquating encroachment of the obsolescence mentality and opening new areas for human living and achievement. Because we are human, increased longevity must be balanced by extended creativity for our sakes and for those who follow us.

A New Environment for Aging Needed

The percentage of older people in the population is growing. Their life expectancy and health are also increasing and improving; and their capacities for intelligence, adaptation, and continued usefulness are available to themselves and society. These three observations make imperative a greater use by society of the resources of so large and creative a proportion of our population. While our technology prolongs life, the creativity of persons sixty-five and older is often not stimulated and utilized.

Social and economic conditions have adverse effects on aging. Our present rate of inflation, social security inequities, and reluctance to employ older people causes desperate financial conditions for many of them and add to their sense of rejection and hopelessness.

Most researchers are agreed that the intellectual and social environments of the elderly are equally impoverished. Family settings and institutions for the aged fail to provide conditions conducive to intellectual growth. The educational system discourages participation by the elderly and focuses instead on the young. Some young people work against their own future by maintaining a negative view of old age which often leads them to withhold assistance for competence in the elderly, or even to punish such competence. How natural it is, therefore, for older persons to accept the stereotypes prepared for them, view themselves as deficient and useless, and put aside intellectual and social performance as a personal goal. Under these conditions deficiencies of all kinds among the aged are a self-fulfilling result.

Educators have not made the same massive efforts to improve the conditions of the aged as they have made to help the young child through government funded programs to overcome learning difficulties. The increasing loss of manpower and creativity that is present in the elderly requires that compensatory educational programs be provided for them. No matter how creative a single elderly person may be he cannot help being affected by the negative conditions that beset the older citizen. A joint effort by individuals, industry, government, and society in general is needed to correct an impoverishing condition for us all. To our concern for conservation of natural resources needs to be added concern for the conservation of some of our richer personal resources.

While results of research are not conclusive about the potentialities of the older person, they are encouraging, and they justify not only education but all kinds of support programs to turn the tide of attitude from a negative view of aging to a positive one. There is abundant evidence that social goals and expectations of society have as much effect on the elderly as on the young. The deleterious effects of these expectations on the aged have been noted and should be eliminated.

In 1971 an American Psychological Association's task force on aging made some specific recommendations for eliminating the unnecessary decline in intellectual and emotional functioning. They recommended, among other things, more forceful implementation of educational programs, innovative programs of voluntary rather than mandatory retirement, second career training, leisure time activity, and more intelligent and efficient utilization of skills that are unaffected by age.

In addition, local communities could enlist the aid of older persons to develop programs that would bring together talented and able elderly people whose services would be used in the accomplishment of needed work in the various aspects of community life. Much important work is left undone because manpower for it is otherwise not available or cannot be afforded. Those in more advanced years could be enlisted to do such work either for some compensation or for the satisfaction of having something to do that would increase their sense of usefulness and self-respect.

Under present negative conditions of neglect and ignominy, many of our older people can be regarded as heroes of our western society. In spite of these conditions many face with courage the maintenance of their powers and the pursuit of their pilgrimage.

I cannot refrain from giving praise to an organization I joined two years ago, The American Association of Retired Persons, which, with its sister organization, The National Retired Teacher's Association, is the largest alliance of older people in the United States, boasting over five million members. They provide an impressive array of services for their members who are fifty-five years or older, such as adult education courses in a great variety of fields. The programs are designed to keep older people interested, intellectually active, and responsive to the world around them. It actively opposes mandatory retirement, lobbies for reform of the social security system, and is a power in the national capital in legislation that affects the well-being and future of older people.

They, with the Gray Panthers, an organization made up of both old and young people, are combining to fight the "throw-away" practices in relation to older people. The obsolescence policy of industry, in this day of growing shortages, has proven costly. Similarly the obsolescent attitude toward the older segment of our society is costly and must be eradicated in our personnel practices. The Center for Democratic Institutions in Santa Barbara predicts that by the year 2000 half of the population will be over 50, and one third over 65. Failure to use the experiences, intelligence, and wisdom of so many older people can become a tragedy for both the aged and for society as a whole.

So learn to love growing older, and to love being older. We, young and old, have an improving future. We can make it increasingly possible to stay young while growing older. No matter how old we are, it is not too late to grow.

11

Exit With Trust

Sometimes when I am concluding a service of worship I suggest to the people, just before the benediction, that they turn and look at the door of the church building through which they will soon pass on their way to their homes. Then I ask: "Think to yourself: Is that door a door of entrance or of exit?" The answer each person gives to himself makes a difference. If the answer is "exit" then there is no future. They will leave behind them whatever meaning the worship had for them. If the answer is "entrance" then they are taking the meaning of the worship experience with them and entering with trust into the world outside.

This is the way I feel about death. I look at that door and ask myself, "Is it an exit or an entrance?" My feelings in response to the question vary. Sometimes when life weighs heavily and despondency—which can accumulate with the

161

years—drags my spirit down, I see death as a welcome exit, an escape from the intolerabilities of life. At other times, the meanings of my life make death seem like a door of entrance through which the self I have been able to grow will pass to a new stage of pilgrimage. Then that door is both a door of exit from this part of my pilgrimage and a door of entrance to the next part.

My training for "exiting with trust" comes out of my own struggle. For example, I have written several versions of this chapter. Each one expressed an earnest sharing of my deepest meanings, but my critics helped me see that what I thought was good and authentic was not good enough. My first response was hurt and anger because the criticism felt like rejection. But instead of responding to those criticisms with hostility and defensiveness, my trust in my critics and in what I was trying to say enabled me to go through a kind of death in relation to what I had created. On the other side of that "door" I now find myself able to make another attempt to express my convictions about exiting with trust with a greater sense of possibility. I cannot be sure, but hopefully my acceptance of the death of one form of my thought will be replaced by a more understandable and helpful form. This is what I mean by "exit with trust."

Jane C., twenty-six, is recovering from an operation following an injury to her back. She is depressed because she can no longer engage in the many sports she previously enjoyed. She said, "I am old. I am finished, I can't do anything." She feels that an important part of her life is dead. The question is, "Can she go through that door in her life's experience as only an exit or can she turn it into an entrance?" Continued depression will only complicate her condition and her relationships with husband, children, and others. If, on the other hand, she can say yes to the change in her life and go through that door, she will be able to use her spirit and strength to heal, discover how well she can overcome her handicap, learn compensations, and discover new capacities. Learning to go through her present "death" with trust will prepare her for the final death when all powers will be taken from her, but she will go with a stronger sense of self and trust.

Mr. and Mrs. James B., aged sixty-five and sixty-three, were a long time deciding whether they would take their first trip to Europe. They wanted to go but were also afraid to go. After weeks of pro and con discussion, they finally made their reservations. Then their anxieties really surfaced! Who could they get to look after their house during their absence? Suppose someone broke into the house and either stole or smashed things. What if one or both became ill during the trip? Would they find adequate help? How would they manage communications when they spoke only English? Would they like their reservations? Could they manage connections from place to place? Several times they almost cancelled the trip because the security of home looked better than ever, and the uncertainties and insecurities of travel were alarming.

They, too, had a "door" problem. Was the act of going on the trip only an exit from the security of home or could they accept it as a door of entrance into an unknown but possibly new and exciting addition to the life they had already lived. They finally decided to make it a door of entry and off they went on their trip. How grateful they were when they returned that they had risked going through that door.

This again is an illustration of my theme: risking and dying to what we have for what more may be is a way of preparing oneself for the death that marks the end of this phase of life.

Why is it so hard to accept death as a part of living? Why

do we have to disguise it, hide the fact of dying from the dying, thus depriving them of a right to participate in their death as a part of life? Why do we hide it from children? Why do we fictionalize death in ways that only complicate children's lives and cause later attitudes toward death that are more fearful than they need be?

I believe the answer lies in our failure to recognize dying as an accompanying experience to living, and the recognition that acceptance of loss, bereavement, failure, and all other threats to being can lead to an emergence into a new, more exciting, fuller and more profound experience of living. If we do not grow a faith in the full experience of living, we have no faith for either psychological, social, economic or physical death.

Because I was born to live and to choose to risk its pain and blessing, I want to choose to live my death with the same deliberate choice as characterized by my living. This seems appropriate because death is a part of my life and without death I cannot know and love life. I want my relationship with death to be as personal as my relationship with life. Thus will I complete my cycle. Then, I will be glad to have lived. But how does one enter into a chosen personal relationship with death?

We have two fears: The fear of life and the fear of death. The fear of life often keeps us from being as heroic as we might be. We tend to draw back from relationships and opportunities as Mr. and Mrs. James B. were tempted to do. Their fear of death—loss of property, health, and security— tempted them not to risk taking the trip and discovering a world that lay on the yonder side of the risk. They dressed up their fear in all kinds of rationalizations about why they ought not to take the trip. Jane faces the same two fears. Will she surrender (give up) to her fear that she is finished and doomed to be prematurely old, or will she surrender (give herself) to the possibility of life. If she chooses the latter she may discover that dying to what was is a way of discovering what can be.

Thus my answer to the two fears of life and death is surrender; not in the sense of giving up, but in the sense of giving oneself to whatever happens—life or death—in the faith that life is the destiny.

Mrs. Philip (Esther) P. learned without warning from her lawyer that her husband had filed for divorce after twenty-eight years of marriage. Two of her three children were grown and married, the third was 18 and finishing high school. Esther had been thinking how free she and Philip would be when Jennie, the youngest, went to college in the fall. Now her dreams were shattered. She soon learned that Philip had fallen in love with a younger woman who worked in the same office where he worked. Anger followed disbelief; then came an attempt to reconstruct their relationship which failed. Next came depression with all the attendant feelings of unattractiveness, rejection, low self-esteem, hurt, loss of interest and indifference. She could not respond to the love and care of friends. Divorce for her was not only the end of a relationship, but the end of trust, hope, and all sense of a future. Divorce and death seemed synonymous.

Divorce was the door! Would it be a door of exit or of entrance? So hurt was she that she was tempted to give up, to quit, to die as an escape. Instead, she decided that she would accept the death that divorce meant to her but move through it to whatever future there might be for her. She accepted the risk implicit in accepting the death of divorce—the risk that there was more for her. To some extent she died to her self-protective concerns and was able to commit herself to try living more openly and deeply. If she had said,

"I loved and was betrayed, I shall never love or trust again," she would have made divorce a door of exit. But moving through that door with faith and heroically building a new life opens possibilities of self-actualization that are immeasurable. Best of all, out of the struggle might be born a sense of self and faith that is triumphant.

Having consented to experiences of dying as a part of living, I must now, as I draw nearer to the end of my life, give myself to death which I view as an old acquaintance in a new form. Being able to look back over my life and seeing that it was good for me to have died to many values for greater ones, I can look into the blank face of death (the face of death is always blank because it reveals nothing and promises nothing) with expectations that beyond this experience in life there will again appear a new good. As I hand over my life, the meaning of it and the value of it, I tremble with both dread and anticipation. But the meanings that we gather from the past experiences of death give us courage in the present to risk the unknown of future death.

Those who have lived heroically, may hope to die heroically. Heroism is the act of overcoming fear. It is the act of trust, based on the hypothesis or faith that the self will be triumphant only after it has affirmed itself by absorbing the negations of the self. What does this mean?

Let me use the common experience of being rejected as an illustration. I went to a party where I was ignored by both host and hostess. I had looked forward to being welcomed as an invited and desired guest; I experienced rejection. My hosts seemed to be saying to me, "You are of no worth. We do not want you here." My self-doubt which always travels with me was activated. I experienced their behavior toward me as negation of my self, my being. I was hurt and shaken.

Gradually I came to myself, however, and realized that I had inner power to affirm myself in spite of outer appraisal.

To do this I had to let go of my egocentric armor that hid my fear and vulnerabilities from me. Then I can say, as Jane C. and Esther P. might say and as Mr. and Mrs. James B. said: "I am who I am. I am my own true self, a center of being and of power. I hurt, but I am more than my hurt; I am afraid but I am more than what I fear; I may respond defensively but I am more than my defensive response." I can refuse to be the victim of negations of myself; instead I may use fears, hurts, injustices and all negations of myself as the fertilizers for the growing of myself. This kind of dealing with negation is what I mean by heroism of living which prepares one for the heroism of dying. This is the courage to be which confronts and accepts the threats to be; including the threat of death and dying.

I am now spelling out more fully what I meant by the death-life-death-life rhythm of our pilgrimage in chapter 2. As I accept each death experience I grow in my power to accept and absorb the negations and denials of self whether they come from the world outside or from within my own soul. I need that strength of self to face my death, just as I need the accumulated wisdom of my years to take with me into the final living of my death.

I have lived this rhythm sometimes with protest and heaviness of heart; at other times with a consenting and buoyant one. I protested being challenged to surrender my illusions about myself. One by one life knocked them down and prevented me from leaning on the illusions others had about me. These pretenses and myths about my self were hard to surrender. But as I lost them I began to find my real self whom I could truly love, and who had lain dormant under all the make-believe I had carried with me. Now I am better able to see through the illusions about others to the heart of others. Sometimes I am able to help them find their own true self by being able to see their true self which has been invisible and unknown to them. The death of the "fabricated" or "made" self and the appearance of the true self is for me an anticipation of the final death and birth.

I began to learn this understanding of death in life, and life in death rhythm many years ago when I was visiting with a dying man. He had put all his affairs in order and was waiting for the end. He was alone and I sat with him. Among other things he said, "This is a strange moment for me. I knew someday this moment would come and I wondered how it would be. I am content, it is good. I am prepared."

I asked what he meant. He continued, "I know what death is like because I have experienced it often. There seemed to be the collapse and the end of things I had built, and of relationships and opportunities. But if I accepted them not as the end but as a door to pass through, I found life on the other side, much more life than I expected. My experience of death and life has prepared me. I exit with trust."